S. Hrg. 114–714

# THE PERSISTENT THREAT OF NORTH KOREA AND DEVELOPING AN EFFECTIVE U.S. RESPONSE

## HEARING

BEFORE THE

### SUBCOMMITTEE ON EAST ASIA, THE PACIFIC AND INTERNATIONAL CYBERSECURITY POLICY

OF THE

## COMMITTEE ON FOREIGN RELATIONS

## UNITED STATES SENATE

ONE HUNDRED FOURTEENTH CONGRESS

SECOND SESSION

SEPTEMBER 28, 2016

Printed for the use of the Committee on Foreign Relations

Available via the World Wide Web:
http://www.fdsys.gpo.gov

U.S. GOVERNMENT PUBLISHING OFFICE

27–084 PDF　　　WASHINGTON : 2017

CONTENTS

-------

# THE PERSISTENT THREAT OF NORTH KOREA AND DEVELOPING AN EFFECTIVE U.S. RESPONSE

## WEDNESDAY, SEPTEMBER 28, 2016

U.S. SENATE,
SUBCOMMITTEE ON EAST ASIA, THE PACIFIC, AND
INTERNATIONAL CYBERSECURITY POLICY,
COMMITTEE ON FOREIGN RELATIONS,
*Washington, DC.*

The subcommittee met, pursuant to notice, at 10:03 a.m. in Room SD–419, Dirksen Senate Office Building, Hon. Cory Gardner, chairman of the subcommittee, presiding.

Present: Senators Gardner [presiding], Rubio, Johnson, Barrasso, Cardin, Udall, Menendez, and Markey.

## OPENING STATEMENT OF HON. CORY GARDNER, U.S. SENATOR FROM COLORADO

Senator GARDNER. This hearing will come to order.

Let me welcome you all to the seventh hearing for the Senate Foreign Relations Subcommittee on East Asia, the Pacific, and International Cybersecurity Policy in the 114th Congress.

As always, I want to thank Senator Cardin for his cooperation and support for holding this important hearing. He has got a busy job on this committee, and it is much appreciated.

This committee has done a great amount of work on North Korea. Thank you to Senator Menendez and Senator Cardin and my colleagues, all of us for the work that we have done on North Korea.

North Korea just conducted its fifth nuclear test, which is the regime's fourth since 2009. It is the regime's second test this year and the largest weapon they have ever tested yet, with an estimated explosive yield of 10 kilotons of TNT.

The rapid advancement of North Korea's nuclear and ballistic missile program represents a grave threat to global peace and stability and a direct threat to the United States homeland in the immediate future.

While failure to stop Pyongyang has been a bipartisan venture over the last 20 years, this administration's policy of strategic patience, crafted under Secretary of State Hillary Clinton, has resulted in the most rapid advancements in North Korea's arsenal of mass destruction.

As the "Washington Post" editorialized on February 9th, 2016, President Obama's policy since 2009, strategic patience, has failed.

The policy has mostly consisted of ignoring North Korea while mildly cajoling China to pressure the regime.

We are now witnessing the consequences of that failure. Nuclear experts have reported that North Korea may currently have as many as 20 nuclear warheads and has the potential to possess as many as 100 warheads within the next 5 years. Director of National Intelligence James Clapper has stated in his testimony to Congress that North Korea has also expanded the size and sophistication of its ballistic missile forces from close-range ballistic missiles to intercontinental ballistic missiles and is committed to developing a long-range nuclear-armed missile that is capable of posing a direct threat to the United States.

This regime is one of the world's foremost abusers of human rights and maintains a vast network of political prison camps where as many as 200,000 men, women, and children are confined to atrocious living conditions and are tortured, maimed, and killed. On February 7th, 2014, the United Nations Human Rights Commission of Inquiry found that North Korea's abuses constituted a crime against humanity.

We also know that Pyongyang is quickly developing its cyber capabilities, as demonstrated by the Sony Pictures hack in 2014 and the repeated attacks on the South Korean financial and communication systems. According to a recent report by the Center for Strategic International Studies, North Korea is emerging as a significant actor in cyberspace with both its military and clandestine organizations gaining the ability to conduct cyber operations.

So given the record of aggression from North Korea and the fecklessness of this administration's policy, this Congress came together on February 10th, 2016 to pass the North Korea Sanctions Policy and Enhancement Act. This legislation, which President Obama signed into law, on February 18th, 2016 was a momentous achievement, the first time ever Congress imposed standalone mandatory sanctions on North Korea. This legislation was also an implicit recognition from the administration that strategic patience has failed and it was time for a new policy of strength.

Now that we are more than 6 months out from the Enhancement Act becoming law, I hope to hear from the administration today regarding its record of compliance with the law. We know that nearly 90 percent of North Korea's trade is with China, and I also hope to hear today from our witnesses a detailed examination of the Peoples Republic of China's record of compliance with U.N. Security Council resolutions regarding North Korea, whether Beijing has utilized any loopholes to avoid faithful compliance and what the United States has done about it.

Sanctions, however, are not the only tool in our arsenal to deal with Pyongyang. First and foremost, we must reassure our allies in South Korea and Japan that aggression against our allies will result in unwavering diplomatic and military support from the United States. As Secretary Ash Carter stated on September 9th, 2016 to his Republic of Korea's counterpart, the United States and the Department of Defense are standing guard 24/7 to deter and defend against the North Korean threat with all aspects of our extended deterrent capabilities, including conventional capabilities, missile defense, and the nuclear umbrella. We must repeat these assurances often to our allies and back them up with actions.

We must continue with the show of force exercises near North Korea to demonstrate to the regime that it will bear a heavy price for any aggression. The B–1 nuclear bomber overflights last month were a good start, and it is my hope that these actions will be consistent and unambiguous in their intent.

We must expedite the placement of terminal high altitude area defense, or THAAD, in the Republic of Korea. And I want to thank our partners in Seoul for their decisiveness and commitment to this critical capability, especially in light of the pressure from Beijing and Moscow.

We must strengthen and build a genuine and lasting trilateral alliance between the United States, Seoul, and Tokyo. There have been encouraging signs, including closer high-level diplomatic consultations and even joint missile defense exercises. I thank both Seoul and Tokyo for wisely pursuing this path of cooperation and partnership.

We must also explore possibilities for asymmetrical actions to put additional pressure on the regime, such as the redesignation of North Korea as a state sponsor of terror, stripping Pyongyang of its United Nations seat or imposing a genuine and enforceable global trade embargo on Pyongyang.

The gravity of the North Korean threat necessitates these conversations, both to guide the actions of this administration, as well as to set parameters for the next administration.

With that, I yield to my good friend and colleague, Senator Cardin.

## STATEMENT OF HON. BENJAMIN L. CARDIN,
## U.S. SENATOR FROM MARYLAND

Senator CARDIN. Well, Senator Gardner, first of all, thank you for calling this hearing. It has been a pleasure to work with you during this Congress on the subcommittee. Clearly, North Korea presents one of our greatest challenges.

To our two witnesses, I thank you. I know that we had to adjust schedules, and thank you very much for being willing to be here today to share your vision as to how we could be more effective in regards to our policies concerning North Korea.

This committee has taken action, as the chairman has indicated, and Congress has passed legislation giving additional tools to the administration to deal with the activities of North Korea, including its most recent tests.

The United Nations has taken action. They have passed Security Council Resolution 2270, and it was our hope that China, working with the Republic of Korea, the United States, Japan, and others in the international community, that we would be able to put sufficient pressure on North Korea to change its behavior. That has not happened. So despite all of our efforts, the current policy is not deterring North Korea's activities in acquiring greater nuclear weapon capacity.

So the question today is what more do we do. How can the administration, working with Congress, provide the leadership internationally to change North Korea's activities?

We know we need to have more effective action by China. What will it take to get China to really exercise the leverage it has over North Korea to change that behavior?

North Korea's current trend presents not just a security challenge to the Korean Peninsula, not just a security challenge to that region of the world, but directly to the United States. What plans do we have in order to protect the security of our allies, as well as our own security, as a result of North Korea's activities?

These are questions that we want to explore today, and we have two incredibly talented people who have given public service over a long period of time. We thank both of you for that, and we look forward to sharing your observations as to what we can do to prevent North Korea from destabilizing that region and presenting a security threat to the United States.

Senator GARDNER. Thank you, Senator Cardin.

And again, thank you to the witnesses for being here. I would ask our distinguished witnesses to keep their oral remarks to no more than 5 minutes. Your full remarks will be entered into the record.

Our first witness is the Honorable Daniel R. Russel who serves as the Assistant Secretary of State for East Asian and Pacific Affairs. Mr. Russel?

## STATEMENT OF HON. DANIEL R. RUSSEL, ASSISTANT SECRETARY OF STATE, BUREAU OF EAST ASIAN AND PACIFIC AFFAIRS, U.S. DEPARTMENT OF STATE, WASHINGTON, D.C.

Mr. RUSSEL. Chairman Gardner, Ranking Member Cardin, members of the subcommittee, thank you for holding this very timely hearing on North Korea. And thank you also for your consistent bipartisan support of U.S.-Asia policy.

The threat from North Korea's missile programs has posed a serious challenge to the last four administrations. Today we are using all of the tools at our disposal, including tools that the Congress has made available to us, to counter that threat and to roll it back. Our strategy is based on deterrence, on diplomacy, and on pressure.

We deter North Korea through a strong defensive military posture rooted in our alliances with South Korea and Japan, and we have strengthened our alliances and our defense cooperation with both those countries to an unprecedented degree. We have expanded our deployments, our exercises, and our weapon systems in order to meet the growing threat.

Diplomatically we have united the world so that North Korea is denied regular access to the international system, so that North Korea is isolated and is widely condemned. But at the same time, we continue to make clear to the North that we are ready at any time to engage in credible negotiations on denuclearization and to offer a path to security, to prosperity, respect, a path that others like Burma have chosen to take.

The third component of our strategy has been pressure, and the tremendous pressure that we have applied through both multilateral and national sanctions has generated serious headwinds for the DPRK regime and significantly impeded its ability to generate desperately needed hard currency, to proliferate arms or nuclear material, to attract international investment or economic assistance, or to extract concessions and aid from the outside world.

Together with our partners in response to the latest nuclear and ballistic missile tests, we will develop a new U.N. Security Council resolution that squeezes North Korea even harder. Together we will expand and coordinate our unilateral sanctions and impose escalating costs on North Korea until it agrees to negotiations on denuclearization and to comply with its international obligations and commitments. Together we will shine a light on the egregious human rights violations and push for accountability by the DPRK's leaders. Together we will defend ourselves and our allies against North Korea's threatening behavior and make clear that there is a high price to pay for provocations.

Mr. Chairman, our strategy has ensured that Kim Jong-un has nothing to show for his intransigence. Yes, he has made holes in the ocean with missiles. Yes, he has detonated nuclear devices in holes in the ground. These are bad things. But it has netted him nothing in terms of what North Korea has indicated that it needs, respect, security, economic support, diplomatic recognition. He has failed to extract material or political benefits from his threats. As President Obama has made clear, we will not reward bad behavior and we will use all the instruments of national power to defend our homeland and our allies against threats from North Korea.

It may well be that negotiating an end to his nuclear program is the last thing on earth that Kim Jong-un wants to do, but if so, we are determined to show him that denuclearization is the only viable option available, that only negotiations offer him a pathway out of danger and isolation.

So I thank the committee for your attention to this critical challenge and, with your permission, would turn to my colleague, Dan Fried. Thank you.

Senator GARDNER. Thank you, Secretary Russel.

Our second witness is Ambassador Daniel Fried who serves as Coordinator for Sanctions Policy at the State Department, a position he has held since January of 2013. Prior, Ambassador Fried served in a various distinguished positions, including Assistant Secretary of State for European Affairs, as Special Assistant to the President, and Senior Director for European and Eurasian Affairs at the National Security Council, and also as United States Ambassador to Poland.

Welcome, Ambassador Fried, and thank you for your service. I look forward to your testimony this morning.

## STATEMENT OF HON. DANIEL FRIED, COORDINATOR FOR SANCTIONS POLICY, U.S. DEPARTMENT OF STATE, WASHINGTON, D.C.

Ambassador FRIED. Thank you, Chairman Gardner, Ranking Member Cardin.

I will continue where my colleague left off. Sanctions are a key component of our strategy, and the sanctions applied to North Korea to date have created significant problems for the regime. Because sanctions work over time as their impact accumulates, the administration, in close coordination with key allies, is examining our sanctions toolkits and identifying ways to prove their efficacy.

We are working through the U.N. with our allies and nationally. And this year has been a year of intensifying pressure in all three areas.

Security Council resolutions play an important role because they have the power to impose universally binding sanctions. The five previous Security Council resolutions on North Korea between 2006 and 2013 targeted North Korea's missile and nuclear programs. They did what they did, but their targets were narrowly focused.

In March 2016, after the January 2016 nuclear test, U.N. Security Council Resolution 2270 imposed, for the first time, measures targeting economic activities generally that supported the Kim regime broadly, not just revenue streams directly connected to nuclear and ballistic missile programs. This is the first time the U.N., with the support of all the Security Council permanent members, including China, took this step. That crossed a line in a good way.

In addition, Congress and the administration, especially after the January 2016 nuclear test, worked together to adopt broad domestic authorities that operate on the principle of that we must go after the revenue streams that support the North Korean regime. And sanctions, as the saying is, as used to be said in Washington, follow the money. The North Korea Sanctions and Policy Enhancement Act was signed by President Obama. We have vigorously used its principles and requirements. The administration has implemented the act including by designating Kim Jong-un himself. Most recently on September 26th, the Treasury Department designated four Chinese nationals and one entity complicit in sanctions evasion activities consistent with the mandatory sanctions in the act. That was a significant and hopefully effective step.

Working with our partners and allies around the world, especially South Korea, Australia, and Japan and increasingly the European Union, we are encouraging and pushing, when necessary, third countries to curtail their own economic ties with North Korea. We have had some good results. We have essentially shut down the operations of North Korean Ocean Maritime Management Company, its shipping line. We have restricted the landing privileges of Air Koryo. Several governments around the world have imposed visa restrictions on North Korean passport holders. South Korea closed the Kaesong Industrial Park in February 2016. Taiwan has halted its imports of North Korean coal. There is more to say about this.

But there is also more to do. China is, by far, North Korea's major economic partner, and North Korea's coal exports mostly to China generate over $1 billion in revenue for the regime annually and account for about a third of all North Korean export income. We are working to curtail North Korea's ability to export coal and iron ore and limit its foreign currency earnings. We are also looking at North Korea's export of labor which provides a source of revenue for the regime.

Secretary Kerry affirmed last week at the UNGA that every country has a responsibility to vigorously enforce U.N. sanctions so that North Korea pays a price for its dangerous activities. We intend to pursue a global pressure campaign on North Korea more generally and to urge, where necessary push, other countries to join that effort. And I look forward to discussing this further with you.

[The joint prepared statement of Ambassador Fried and Assistant Secretary Russel follows:]

JOINT PREPARED STATEMENT OF AMBASSADOR DANIEL FRIED
AND ASSISTANT SECRETARY DANIEL RUSSEL

### INTRODUCTION

Chairman Gardner, Ranking Member Cardin, and members of the subcommittee, thank you for the opportunity to appear before you today to testify about the U.S. response to the threat from North Korea.

### THE CHALLENGE POSED BY A BELLIGERENT NORTH KOREA

The continued development of North Korea's nuclear and ballistic missile programs is a threat to the United States homeland, our allies, and the peace, security, and stability of the region. Two nuclear tests and an unprecedented series of ballistic missile launches this year flagrantly violate United Nations Security Council Resolutions (UNSCRs). Moreover, North Korea has repeatedly threatened to attack the United States and our allies with nuclear weapons.

The threats have become more frequent and the rhetoric more alarming. Mere days ago, North Korea's foreign minister delivered a defiant speech to the U.N. General Assembly, stating that the United States will "face consequences beyond imagination" from North Korea. During August's annual military exercise with the Republic of Korea (ROK) and following the announcement of the planned deployment of the Terminal High Altitude Aerial Defense (THAAD) system, Pyongyang explicitly warned of pre-emptive nuclear strikes against the United States and our allies.

Significant advances in North Korea's nuclear weapons and ballistic missiles programs underpin this bellicosity. These programs are funded at the cost of the well-being of the North Korean people, who suffer economic deprivation and horrific human rights abuses at the hands of the Kim Jong Un regime.

### OUR COMPREHENSIVE NORTH KOREA POLICY

The goal of our policy towards North Korea is the denuclearization of the Korean Peninsula in a peaceful manner. The North Korea itself committed to this goal in the September 19, 2005 Joint Statement of the Six-Party Talks. However, since making that pledge, North Korea abandoned the Six-Party Talks, rejected negotiations on denuclearization, and conducted five nuclear tests and a series of ballistic missile launches, in flagrant violation of its international obligations and commitments.

Our policy is grounded in three tracks: deterrence, pressure, and diplomacy. It seeks to convince Pyongyang to return to the negotiating table and agree to complete, verifiable, and irreversible denuclearization.

To deter a North Korean attack, we maintain a strong defensive military posture, rooted in our ironclad alliances with the ROK and Japan. We consistently and publicly reaffirm our commitment to our Allies and continue to work with the ROK and Japan to develop a comprehensive set of Alliance capabilities to counter the multiple threats, including in particular the North Korean ballistic missile threat.

We have pursued a comprehensive, sustained pressure campaign - of which sanctions are a key part. The goal of this pressure is to raise the cost to North Korea for violating international law and to impede the North's ability to participate in or to fund its unlawful activities. We are steadily tightening sanctions in an effort to compel the Kim regime to return to credible negotiations on denuclearization by targeting the regime's revenue and reputation.

We have made repeated diplomatic overtures to North Korea signaling our commitment to the 2005 Joint Statement and our willingness to engage in credible and authentic talks aimed at restarting negotiations on denuclearization. We also are engaged in diplomatic effort to build more rigorous and universal enforcement of Resolution 2270's sanctions measures, and to block illicit North Korean WMD and proliferation-related actions.

North Korea views diplomatic meetings and visits as important markers of its international legitimacy. This month, we instructed our embassies around the world to ask host governments to condemn the test and take further additional actions to downgrade or sever diplomatic and economic ties. As of September 25, 75 countries have issued statements condemning the test and several others have cancelled or downgraded planned meetings or visits with officials from North Korea.

### SANCTIONS AS A FOREIGN POLICY TOOL

Sanctions are an important component of our strategy for impeding the DPRK's unlawful programs and, ultimately, compelling it to negotiate a freeze, rollback, and elimination of its nuclear program. The sanctions applied to date have created significant problems for the North Korean regime, but they have not yet caused the DPRK to change course. The Administration in close coordination with our key allies is continually examining our sanctions toolkit and identifying ways to improve their efficacy.

North Korea poses particular challenges from a sanctions perspective, given its relative economic isolation. Unlike Iran, whose mid-sized economy was predicated on an industry that needed access to the international financial system, North Korea is one of the least developed economies on the planet. The country prides itself on an ideology which values self-reliance above all. This isolation and economic immaturity preclude a sanctions response based solely on U.S. domestic authorities.

North Korea's economy is heavily dependent on China. The Administration has engaged Beijing at the highest levels to seek greater Chinese cooperation is imposing costs on North Korea for its threatening behavior. We regularly urge China to do more to prevent North Korea from using Chinese companies or infrastructure in ways that can benefit the DPRK's illicit activities. We have also taken a number of actions in conjunction with partners around the world to close off revenue streams from outside China.

### MULTILATERAL SANCTIONS THROUGH U.N. SECURITY COUNCIL RESOLUTIONS

UN Security Council Resolutions have played an important role in our pressure campaign on North Korea, because they have the power to impose universally binding sanctions. The five UNSCRs on North Korea (1695, 1718, 1874, 2087, and 2094) adopted between 2006 and 2013 target North Korea's missile and nuclear programs. While these resolutions have an impact, their targets were narrowly focused.

However, in March 2016, UNSCR 2270 imposed for the first time measures targeting economic activities that support the Kim regime broadly, not just revenue streams directly connected to the nuclear and ballistic missile programs. UNSCR 2270 includes unprecedented inspection and financial provisions, including mandatory inspections of cargo to and from North Korea, and a requirement to terminate banking relationships with North Korean financial institutions.

In order to maximize global implementation of UNSCR 2270, the Administration has strengthened efforts to provide information and expertise to the Security Council's North Korea Sanctions Committee and its Panel of Experts. We continue to engage in vigorous outreach to member states to highlight these new international obligations, build capacity globally, and bring attention to implementation gaps.

### U.S. AUTHORITIES AND OTHER NATIONAL SANCTIONS

In the wake of the January 2016 nuclear test, Congress and the Administration worked together to adopt broad domestic authorities that operate on the principle that we must go after all revenue streams that support the Kim regime. The North Korea Sanctions and Policy Enhancement Act (NKSPEA or the Act) was signed by President Obama in February 2016.

In the seven months since its enactment, the Administration has been vigorously implementing the Act.

- March 15: The President issues EO 13722, which implements aspects of NKSPEA. The Treasury Department makes 12 additions to the Specially Designated Nationals (SDN) list, consistent with authorities outlined in NKSPEA. The State Department designates five North Korean individuals and entities under EO (Executive Order) 13382, which targets Weapons of Mass Destruction proliferators and their supporters.

- May 17: The State Department publishes an enhanced travel warning with respect to North Korea.

- June 2: The Treasury Department identifies North Korea as a jurisdiction of primary money laundering concern, and proposes new prohibitions on North Korean banking activity.

- June 9: The State Department transmits a Report to Congress on actions taken to implement the U.S. strategy to improve international implementation of U.N. sanctions on North Korea.
- June 30: The Treasury Department, with support from the State Department and the Office of the Director of National Intelligence, submits a report to Congress on North Korea's activities undermining cybersecurity, as one of a number of reports mandated by the Act. In the report, the State Department outlines the U.S. government's strategy to engage foreign partners to combat such activity.
- July 6: The State Department publishes the NKSPEA-mandated Report to Congress on human rights abuses in North Korea. Based in part on information contained in the report, the Treasury Department makes 16 additions to the SDN list, including Kim Jong Un.
- August 11: The State Department transmits a Report to Congress on U.S. policy toward North Korea based on a complete interagency review of policy alternatives.
- August 24: The State Department transmits a Report to Congress regarding the U.S. strategy to promote initiatives to enhance international awareness and address the human rights situation in North Korea.
- September 1: The State Department transmits a Report to Congress detailing a plan for making unrestricted, unmonitored, and inexpensive mass communication available to the people of North Korea.
- September 26: The Treasury Department designates four Chinese nationals and one entity complicit in sanctions evasion activities, consistent with mandatory sanctions in the Act.

Further, our partners and allies around the world have also implemented their own strong domestic sanctions regimes, going far beyond that required by UNSCRs. These include South Korea, Australia, Japan, Canada, the EU, and other countries.

### PROGRESS

Our diplomatic campaign to leverage UNSCRs, other multilateral efforts, and national authorities has produced results. Recent successes include:

- The operations of North Korea's U.N.-designated shipping line, Ocean Maritime Management Company have been essentially shut down and its ships are denied access to ports, scrapped, impounded, or confined to their homeports.
- Air Koryo's landing privileges at foreign airports have been reduced.
- Several governments have imposed visa restrictions on North Korean passport holders.
- South Korea closed the Kaesong Industrial Park in February 2016, closing off an important source of foreign currency to the regime.
- Bangladesh, South Africa, Burma, and other countries have expelled North Korean diplomats involved in illicit activities.
- Taiwan has halted its imports of North Korean coal.
- Malta ended its visa extensions for North Korean workers.
- Mongolia de-flagged North Korean ships and Cambodia recently instituted rules prohibiting foreign-owned ships from flying the Cambodian flag.
- As recently as June 2016, the State Department used the Iran, North Korea, and Syria Nonproliferation Act (INKSNA) to impose additional sanctions on North Korean persons for their proliferation activities.

### CHALLENGES

There is more to do. North Korea's coal exports, mostly to China, generate over $1 billion in revenue for the regime annually and account for about a third of all export income. We are working to build on previous UNSCRs to address loopholes that allow North Korea to export coal and iron ore, earning precious foreign currency for the Kim regime on the backs of enslaved workers, including children. North Korea's shipping lines limp along, despite years of sanctions and key victories like the seizure of arms aboard the Chong Chon Gang and the impoundment of the Mu Du Bong. North Korea's export of labor continues to provide a source of revenue for the regime.

We are not yet satisfied and believe there is more we can do. Much will depend on China, which is by far North Korea's greatest trading partner. China consistently says that it opposes North Korea's ballistic missile launches and nuclear weapons programs. China has supported the adoption of UNSCRs on North Korea, including UNSCR 2270. China also supported the Security Council's press statement in response to the latest nuclear test, which stated that the Security Council will begin work immediately on sanctions in a new Security Council resolution. Securing increased cooperation and application of pressure on North Korea is a major goal of our diplomacy with China.

We recognize China's concerns that pressure on North Korea could precipitate a crisis, but we point out that its nuclear and missile programs pose a far greater threat to regional security. We acknowledge China's steps to implement U.N. sanctions but repeatedly urge China to improve implementation and apply pressure needed to effect a change in North Korean behavior.

China has objected to U.S. actions intended to strengthen our defenses against North Korean military threats to ourselves and our allies, but we make clear that we will take all necessary steps to deter and defend against those threats. We closely coordinate with China on sanctions and other measures to counter North Korea's problematic behavior, but we have not shied away from unilateral actions against North Korean actors, including those located in China.

CONCLUSION

Today's hearing provides us an opportunity to send a strong, clear message of resolve to hold North Korea accountable to its commitments and international obligations. As Secretary Kerry affirmed at the U.N. General Assembly, every country has a responsibility to vigorously enforce U.N. sanctions to ensure that North Korea "pays a price for its dangerous actions." With the U.N. and our allies, more remains to be done; we intend to pursue the global pressure campaign on North Korea more generally, and to urge, and where necessary push, other countries to join that effort.

Senator GARDNER. Thank you, Ambassador Fried.

We will begin the questions.

I commend the administration for finally designating a Chinese entity and four Chinese individuals this week, as you mentioned in your opening statements, for North Korea sanctions violations. I do wonder, though, if these designations would have taken place without the studies, the groundbreaking work released by the Center for Advanced Defense Studies and the Asian Institute for Policy Studies that publicly identified these very same entities and networks and received widespread media coverage. Would it not have happened without those studies?

Regardless, it is my hope that this action will send a strong message to Beijing and to all of Pyongyang's enablers. It is also important to see the change in the administration's work and policy as a result of the heavy involvement from Congress beginning with the Enhancement Act passage and continued oversight.

This round of designations, though, should only scratch the surface of the eligible violators. In a new study called Stopping North Korea, Incorporated, Harvard and MIT researchers found that the North Korean state trading company's managers have shifted their strategy by, one, hiring more capable Chinese middlemen who can more effectively handle financing, logistics, and doing business with private Chinese firms and foreign firms operating in China; number two, taking up residence and embedding themselves on the mainland, which increases their effectiveness; number three, expanding the use of Hong Kong and Southeast Asian regional commercial hubs; and four, increasing the use of embassies as a vehicle for procurement.

It is my hope that State and Treasury are carefully reviewing the recommendations from both studies and taking appropriate action and strategy adjustments.

So, Ambassador Fried, how many investigations are active and currently ongoing pursuant to the North Korea Sanctions and Policy Enhancement Act?

Ambassador FRIED. We are current, to my knowledge, in providing the mandatory reports in that act. That is, we have sent up all of them that we are required to do so. And frankly, we appreciate the opportunity.

The administration and the Congress are moving in the same direction, and to the degree we send a signal of a united American position, the stronger we all are. So I thank you for that.

The Treasury Department, State Department are active in pursuing a number of potential North Korean targets. My Treasury colleagues are working diligently and may I say aggressively in tracking down violators of sanctions both U.N. sanctions and American sanctions. Parts of the State Department, particularly my colleagues who work on nonproliferation, have their own stream of activities and investigations. They follow arms shipments. They follow ships. They do this in great detail. And I can assure you that they are aggressive. I cannot give you a number of specific investigations, but there are a lot of them. We follow both public material. You mentioned one. There are others. We also use intelligence information. We are in a forward-leaning mode.

Senator GARDNER. And how many of these investigations that are taking place are of Chinese entities or individuals?

Ambassador FRIED. I do not want to get into specific numbers in this session, but let me say this because it is an important question and comes to the heart of the matter. It would be best if China itself came to the conclusion that it needed to put increased pressure on the North. My colleague knows this better than I do, but China has expressed concern about an opposition to North Korea's nuclear testing especially. So the best option is if China does this itself.

It would also be useful if Chinese banks and companies understood that increasingly dealing with North Korean companies, especially those that are sanctioned, is going to be risky, frankly not worth it.

The best sanctions are those that do not have to be applied because the credible threat of sanctions acts as a deterrent.

The U.S. Government's action earlier this week demonstrates that we are in earnest, and I can assure you that we are. There is more we could say in a classified setting, but I think you understand the direction that we are headed.

Senator GARDNER. Let me just ask this before I turn to Senator Cardin. Maybe a simpler way to ask it is, are additional Chinese firms under investigation?

Ambassador FRIED. Treasury and State are investigating a number of companies around the world. I will put it this way. There are no limits and there is no administration redline of exempt countries or companies. We go where the evidence takes us.

Senator GARDNER. And so I think the answer is yes, additional Chinese firms are under investigation.

Ambassador FRIED. I would not argue with you.

Senator GARDNER. Thank you.

Senator Cardin?

12

Senator CARDIN. Well, once again, thank you for your testimony and for your service to our country, both of you.

Secretary Russel, I agree with you that we have done a lot in leadership on imposing global sanctions against the regime in North Korea, and it has had a major economic impact on North Korea. There is no question about that. But it has not worked. It has not worked. North Korea continues to accumulate enriched materials. It continues to nuclearize weapons. It continues to develop delivery systems that could threaten not only the region but the United States.

Ambassador Fried, you mentioned countries that have been very helpful to us, and we appreciate what Australia is doing and the Republic of Korea is doing and Japan is doing, Canada is doing, and now you mentioned even the EU. But it was notable that you did mention China in that list of countries that have gone beyond the U.N. resolution. In fact, China appears to look for ways to weaken the impact of the Security Council resolution.

We know about the livelihood exemption. You mentioned coal exports. You mentioned how dependent North Korea is on the exports of coal. But this is perplexing because China does not want to destabilize the Korean Peninsula and does not want North Korea to have its nuclear arsenal that it has and is growing, and it could do so much more. It could.

So what can the United States do? It is for both of you. What can the United States do to get China to take the steps it could take that will put the type of pressure on North Korea that they will change their behavior in regards to their nuclear program?

Mr. RUSSEL. Well, thank you, Senator Cardin.

I first started working on North Korea 25 years ago under the George H.W. Bush 41 administration and have a healthy appreciation of the challenge that has faced four successive administrations dealing with North Korea and motivating China to cooperate with us. The difference between 25 years ago and today is dramatic. The difference between 8 years ago and today is dramatic in terms of the extent to which China has begun cooperating with the United States in an effort to freeze, roll back, and eliminate North Korea's nuclear and missile programs.

Senator CARDIN. But do you not agree that China could very easily put the type of pressure on North Korea that would change the equation here?

Mr. RUSSEL. We all know—we certainly agree that a change in China's behavior is a prerequisite for getting a change in North Korea's behavior, that China has potentially tremendous leverage over North Korea even though it has relatively little influence.

Senator CARDIN. So what can we do to get China to move? What can we do to get China to move?

Mr. RUSSEL. Well, first, unfortunately, North Korea's actions and increasingly egregious behavior, which we do not like, are generating a change in China's behavior.

Senator CARDIN. What are we seeing that indicates China is changing its fundamental position in regards to North Korea? Coal exports are up. Are they not?

Mr. RUSSEL. China is changing its behavior, not necessarily its fundamental position towards North Korea. And that behavior is manifest in its cooperation with the United States in trying to stem proliferation and trying to enforce resolution 2270 and in creating barriers to North Korean programs.

Senator CARDIN. But when you have the livelihood exemption being interpreted in a way that China is interpreting it, it is a loophole that effectively takes China out of the equation when it comes to putting pressure on North Korea. And without Chinese pressure—we could have the strongest possible sanction regime globally—North Korea is protected.

Mr. RUSSEL. We fully agree that placing restrictions on the DPRK's ability to export coal to China or anywhere else is a priority and it is a focus of the negotiations that are currently underway over a new U.N. Security Council resolution.

Senator CARDIN. Is it correct that North Korea's exports to China have grown by—I have 27.5 percent by value in August, making it the sharpest increase? They are not only not helping us, they are helping North Korea. Are they not?

Mr. RUSSEL. We believe—and President Obama, after meeting with President Xi Jinping, in which he had a very, very direct and forceful exchange on the DPRK and sanctions policy, said publicly that China can and should do more to tighten sanctions. This is a goal of U.S. diplomacy. This is only one facet, however, of China's behavior vis-a-vis the DPRK, and there are significant improvements in China's cooperation with the U.S. and the Republic of Korea in both implementing the 2270 U.N. sanctions and in pushing back against the risk of either provocations or proliferation.

Senator CARDIN. Well, that is a pretty general statement, and I would like to drill down on it. And I will ask that you get our committee information on how China has been so helpful. But it seems to me that because of its economic relationship with North Korea—its economic relationship with North Korea—that all the work we are doing on sanctions globally is being compromised dramatically because of China's economic relationship with North Korea. That does not seem to make any sense.

Mr. RUSSEL. We share the concern, Senator, that China's purchases of coal and other economic activities create a lifeline that reduces the impact of global sanctions, and we are working directly with Chinese senior leadership to encourage and persuade them to tighten up and to toughen up for the purpose of bringing about a change in the DPRK's behavior.

Senator CARDIN. Thank you, Mr. Chairman.

Senator GARDNER. Thank you, Senator Cardin.

It is hard to believe that China is serious about effecting change in North Korea's behavior when they continue to share a billion dollars' worth of coal exports and continue to share 90 percent of their economy. I think Senator Cardin—what he was getting at was Chinese cooperation and are they going to be willing in this new security resolution that you are talking about to narrow or limit the livelihood exemption in the new Security Council resolution that you mentioned several times now.

Mr. RUSSEL. That is what is under negotiation now. We certainly hope so, and we are working to that end. At the same time, we are pursuing law enforcement cooperation and other forms of sanctions enforcement and implementation in an effort to continue to tighten the net on the DPRK for the purpose of changing their behavior and bringing them to real negotiations.

Senator GARDNER. Well, perhaps we can get further into this.

Senator Barrasso?

Senator BARRASSO. Well, thank you very much, Mr. Chairman, for holding this hearing.

And to Senator Cardin, I think you are absolutely right on all of the issues that you have raised. I mean, I think about what is happening. I look at September 9th, 2016, Defense Secretary Carter discussed the most recent nuclear test by North Korea. He says, quote, China has and shares important responsibility for this development and has an important responsibility to reverse it. He goes on and he says, and so it is important that it use its location, its history, its influence to further the denuclearization of the Korean Peninsula and not the direction things have been going.

So I ask you, Assistant Secretary Russel, is China willing to impose any consequences, any additional sanctions against North Korea for this most recent nuclear test? And what specific actions—specific actions because, as Senator Cardin said, you know, we hear kind of general answers. What specific actions did the administration ask China to take in response to these nuclear tests and the missile launches?

Mr. RUSSEL. Thank you, Senator.

I agree 100 percent with what Secretary Carter said.

The President has met repeatedly with President Xi Jinping over the course of 2016, as recently as early this month, in Hangzhou, China, and very forcefully presented our specific asks and recommendations in terms of practical ways that China can enhance the effectiveness of sanctions through border controls, through limiting access to Chinese banks, through limits on Air Koryo and other modes of transportation, shutting down North Korea's cyber bad actors, including on Chinese servers and soil. The list goes on. President Obama met again in New York last week with Premier Li Keqiang and again pushed very forcefully.

We have both a strategic and economic dialogue in which Secretary Kerry with his counterpart, the State Counselor of China, have delved into this. And at every level below that, we have worked directly with China to enhance and improve their cooperation and their implementation.

We are not fully satisfied. There is much more that we believe China can and should do. We look for ways to demonstrate that it is very much in China's interest to do more, and we have demonstrated, including through the decision to deploy the THAAD system, that the United States and our allies will take the steps necessary to protect us against the threat posed by the DPRK even when those steps are unwelcome by the Chinese. We have pointed out that the solution to their concerns about the behavior of the U.S. military in Northeast Asia is for them to act more assertively in changing the DPRK's behavior and ending the missile and nuclear programs.

Senator BARRASSO. Mr. Chairman, what we heard is that the President I think he said pushed forcefully, but it has not been very effective. So I want to talk specifically about trade between

China and North Korea. And, Ambassador, you may want to weigh in on this.

China is North Korea's largest trading partner. China has worked hard to put loopholes, as Senator Cardin referred to, and exemptions to many of the North Korea sanctions at the United Nations Security Council. I mean, that seems to be the way that China is working. There is an exemption under the UNSC Resolution 2270 that allows North Korea to sell coal and iron ore. China continues to import North Korea's coal, iron, iron ore.

So I would ask, Mr. Ambassador, what would be the impact of a complete ban on China's import of North Korea's coal, iron, and iron ore, and is the administration working to this end, to get rid of these loopholes and exemptions?

Ambassador FRIED. Yes, we are, indeed, working to address the problem of North Korean coal exports generally and specifically to China. If in sanctions you follow the money, the money takes you to coal. It also takes you to some other sectors. But your question was to coal, so I will stick with that.

The most effective way would be, of course, to address this through a new UNSCR, a new Security Council resolution. UNSCRs generally are the gold standard because they are universally accepted and legally binding.

If that is not possible, there are other options. We can seek to convince Chinese individual companies that it would be in their own best interest to avoid dealing with the most suspect North Korean coal exporters. And the administration's actions on Monday designating Chinese companies demonstrates that nothing is off limits, including this.

I do not want to get more specific at this point, but the questions from Chairman Gardner and Ranking Member Cardin are exactly the right ones. I take it as a good sign that those are the questions the administration is grappling with right now actively.

Senator BARRASSO. Let me ask a final question. I know my time is expiring.

According to the Congressional Research Service, this year alone, North Korea has conducted almost 30 missile tests, double the number of last year. What are we hearing from our friends in Japan and South Korea about what is happening over there?

Mr. RUSSEL. There is immense and appropriate concern in Japan and in South Korea about the accelerating tempo of North Korea's ballistic missile activity and a commensurate willingness to work closely with the United States to promote military interoperability, information sharing, joint exercises, and a variety of other defense-related programs that are increasing our ability to deter and to defend against this significant threat.

Senator BARRASSO. Thank you, Mr. Chairman.

Senator GARDNER. Senator Menendez? And I want to thank Senator Menendez for his work on the legislation that so much of this hearing is focusing on. Thank you.

Senator MENENDEZ. Well, thank you, Mr. Chairman, for holding the hearing. I want to commend you on your active leadership in this regard. We worked together on the North Korea Sanctions and Policy Enhancement Act, and I appreciate that that is one of the vehicles that we are using to try to push back against North Korea's not only promotion of its nuclear weaponry but also my concern of proliferation as well.

And I think all of my colleagues from what I gather, because I was having meetings in my office but had the TV on, have asked the same questions. What is that we need to do to get China? And I must say that one of the things that I am convinced that we are unwilling to do—and it is from my experience as one of the authors of the Iran Sanctions Act—is to sanction the universe of financial transactions because those would lead to Chinese banks. And when we do that, that had some of the toughest and most consequential actions on Iran.

Now, we have not pursued the financial transactions center as an element of getting those who want to facilitate North Korea's actions and creating pressure on them as the world created pressure on Iran from disengaging with it financially.

So, Ambassador Fried, have we, meaning the administration, contemplated the type of financial sanctions that we levied against Iran as it relates to those who would be doing business with North Korea and who would be permitting them access to their banking centers?

Ambassador FRIED. We are looking at all possible points of leverage and pressure against North Korea and the North Korean economy. We have abundant tools.

You are quite right that the financial sanctions against Iran, combined with the oil and gas sanctions, were powerful. So there is no question about that.

Senator MENENDEZ. I did not ask you about all tools. I am asking specifically about these tools.

It seems to me that we are reticent to pursue the type of financial transactions because they would largely lead to Chinese banks. And so in the absence of doing that, one of the most powerful tools that you might have left to get North Korea to observe international norms and the will of the international community, as expressed by the United Nations, is missing. Why is it that the administration has not come forward and sought specifically that type of either tool or implement it if they think they have the power to do so themselves?

Ambassador FRIED. We actually have sanctioned—we have designated a number of North Korean banks. And the action which the administration took on Monday demonstrates that we are willing to take the next step of designating third country entities which are cooperating with designated North Korean banks. So we have crossed that line, and we are actively looking and constantly looking at additional targets.

Senator MENENDEZ. Which Chinese banks have you sanctioned?

Ambassador FRIED. Well, this Monday, there were Chinese financial institutions sanctioned by the Treasury Department. It was four Chinese nationals and one entity complicit in sanctions evasion.

Senator MENENDEZ. Nationals is good, but I am talking about institutions.

Ambassador FRIED. And an institution. This was a financial institution.

Senator MENENDEZ. Well, I would like to know whether you have all the authorities you need to go after Chinese banks that are engaged in dealing with the financial transactions that North Korea would ultimately need because it seems to me that if we are going after those banks, that that is an incredibly powerful tool. So if you can just explicitly tell me, do you have all the authorities that you need, and if so, is it the intention of the administration to use those authorities against whatever bank, whether they be Chinese or others, as it relates to transactions with North Korea?

Ambassador FRIED. Yes, we believe we have the authorities we need, and yes, we are looking at all possible pressure points, including financial.

Senator MENENDEZ. So if that is the case, then the onus is on the administration, not on Congress, to provide you additional authorities that you obviously do not need based upon your answer.

Let me ask one other question. One of my main concerns is North Korea's level—and, Mr. Secretary, maybe you could speak to this—about sharing and transferring nuclear technology. North Korea has successfully subverted sanctions and export and import controls often through falsely flagging cargo ships. I want to get a sense from you what steps are we taking, what steps our international partners are taking since March to more rigorously monitor and ensure that all countries are complying with the strict controls the U.N. Security Council passed in March.

Mr. RUSSEL. Senator, I would go one step further than merely the U.N. Security Council resolution. Because proliferation is a paramount concern of the Obama administration, we are working through a variety of intelligence and law enforcement channels to significantly enhance the monitoring of DPRK activities to establish telltales and tripwires for the purpose of making it harder and harder for the DPRK to successfully sell or transfer either technology or fissile material and to try to ensure that we are able to detect efforts they may undertake to do that. That involves close cooperation not only with North Korea's neighbors but also ensuring that it is constrained in terms of its ability to move ships, cargo, planes, and people. So increased scrutiny at international airports, greater verification of passport information, the requirement of visas, as well as close government-to-government information sharing are among the steps that we are taking.

If I could add, Senator, to your important point about China. We are working our way through the suite of options in terms of steps that we can take vis-a-vis China's behavior towards North Korea. We have begun, obviously, with the goal of persuading China to take more and more action in part because China can do far more effectively and usefully, from our point of view, willingly than we can achieve indirectly through direct sanctions against China, but we have, as my colleague, Dan Fried, mentioned, not balked at taking direct action against Chinese entities or people when the evidence is there. We make a point of bringing information to the Chinese and encouraging the Chinese to act on that information and to develop it further in their own law enforcement and security channels. They have abundant tools of their own to put restrictions on the DPRK.

I am not in the business of defending China. We think that there is much more that they need to do. As I mentioned, President Obama stood up in China and made that point directly and explicitly in public, as he has in private. But the fact is that the trend line of Chinese action against DPRK proliferation, missile and nuclear activities, and the trend line of China's cooperation with the international community generally through the U.N. and with the United States on a bilateral basis is improving.

Senator GARDNER. Senator Rubio?

Senator RUBIO. Thank you.

Mr. Fried, I want to talk about this report, a recent study by the Center for Advanced Defense Studies. It is called In China's Shadow. And basically it is clear from this report that China has allowed a Chinese company and its front company to conduct about $532 million in trade volume. The report identified six companies. You discussed here the sanctions against one. Why did Treasury only designate one of those six companies?

Ambassador FRIED. We are actively looking at all possible targets. I will not speak for Treasury and its individual decisions, but in my experience, Treasury is both effective and aggressive in identifying targets and pursuing them. We have to have sufficient evidence to meet Treasury's legal threshold. But I will tell you that we are in the mode of gathering information and we will go where the information takes us.

Senator RUBIO. But that just sounds like—I mean, I get it.

Ambassador FRIED. I do not want to talk about a specific company and a specific designation, at least in this session.

Senator RUBIO. Why? They are out there in this report. I mean, they are named. The world and everyone knows who these companies are. There is not a mystery here.

Ambassador FRIED. Well, as a general rule, it is best not to talk about current investigations——

Senator RUBIO. That is true in a court of law.

Ambassador Fried:—in an open session.

Senator RUBIO. No. That is absurd. This is a report that is out there for the world to see. Everyone knows this. This is not a secret.

Ambassador FRIED. I will tell you what. I will consult with my Treasury colleagues and try to get you whatever we can——

Senator RUBIO. And that is why these hearings often—I mean, they are just so hard to sit through sometimes because you just get all this—and I do not mean to be disrespectful. I know you are towing the company line or whatever, the Secretary of State's line on this stuff. But I think everyone can see what this is. I mean, we are afraid to press the case against too many Chinese companies because of the broader situation between China and the United States.

Let me ask you for the record. Has the White House or the State Department ever pressured the Justice Department or Treasury to delay designations and law enforcement actions to avoid embarrassing China?

Ambassador FRIED. Not to my knowledge, no, sir.

Senator RUBIO. Because we have a Department of Justice indictment that was unsealed in civil forfeiture actions. The criminal indictment lists transactions of millions of U.S. dollars going all the way back to 2009 where there were these front companies that served as financial intermediaries for U.S. dollar transactions between North Korean-based entities who were being financed by KKBC, which is a designated North Korean bank, and suppliers in other countries. And it was done in order to evade restrictions on U.S. dollar transactions.

I do not understand. From 2009 to 2016, why did we wait to act against these persons? And the only conclusion one could draw is that beyond the issue of sanctions, we have here the issue of pressure because of the broader situation with China and our foreign policy. And I got to be frank. This just looks to me like an administration that is saying let us not go too hard on some of these Chinese companies because it is going to destabilize our broader relationship with China on a series of other topics. And that is what it looks like.

Here is another point that I do not understand. There are three times as many Iran-related persons designated by the United States than North Korea-related persons. Can anyone describe for me the reason for this discrepancy? I have no problem with there being a lot of Iran-related designations, but why are there so many more Iran-related designations than North Korean-related designations when in fact North Korea has already not only developed weapons but are demonstrating it and using them in all sorts of tests? Why the discrepancy?

Ambassador FRIED. The first point to make is that the administration's action on Monday to designate the Chinese banks was an important step. And as I said earlier in the hearings, we are actively looking at a number of targets.

With respect to the numbers and comparing Iran and North Korea, the Iranian is both much larger and much more connected to the rest of the world than the North Korean economy, and the North Korea economy was—despite huge areas that are hidden beyond the various walls of secrecy in Iran, is generally more open. That may have something to do with the numbers.

But to answer what I think, Senator, is your larger point, the administration shares Congress' view that the North Korean threat and North Korean actions, including especially the recent nuclear tests, compels us to intensify our pressure campaign working both through the U.N. with third countries such as the Japanese, South Koreans, Europeans, Australians, Canadians and using our national authorities in a coordinated fashion to increase the pressure. We welcomed the legislation earlier this year. We have put it to good use, and we intend to pursue North Korean targets aggressively.

Senator RUBIO. All I can say is that what this looks like from watching it is that what we are basically involved in here is a provocation-response cycle with North Korea. And you talk about the sanctions. I know my time is up. And you talk about the bill that Congress passed earlier this year, that we passed this year. But it was only until then that we finally designated North Korea as a primary money laundering concern.

Again, this whole thing looks like to be a combination of things. This provocation cycle that we have gotten ourselves into with

North Korea, we are holding back on sanctions and able to use them if they provoke us in a different setting, and this cycle continues. North Koreans have played this brilliantly over the last few years buying time for themselves to reach the point they have reached.

And the other is, quite frankly, what this looks like is that the United States is holding its diplomatic fire and its sanctions fire on some of these issues for fear of impacting our relationship with China and our fear of offending the Chinese government or going after some of their entities who, by the way, are also involved in all sorts of other endeavors that are questionable.

So, again, Mr. Chairman, I do not know why it has taken so long and why so little has been done. It is no surprise we are at the point we are at today.

Ambassador FRIED. Just one point, Senator. You mentioned—my words, not yours—the trap of the provocation and response cycle. That is not what we are doing. This year especially, working through the U.N. and other channels, we are in a position of intensifying pressure independent of a provocation-response cycle. We are in earnest. We intend to increase pressure on North Korea. To do so, we also have to work around the world with third countries and with the Chinese, as my colleague pointed out. That is our intention. So I agree that a provocation-response cycle and staying within such a cycle would not be the right approach, and that is not our approach.

Mr. RUSSEL. Mr. Chairman, with your permission, I would just add, Senator Rubio, that if it were the administration's policy to tiptoe around China in dealing with the North Korean threat, we would never have decided with the Republic of Korea to deploy the THAAD system. We would never have designated a Chinese entity and Chinese national. We would never have taken the decision to send a B–1 bomber or aircraft carrier to the Korean Peninsula.

It is very much the case that we seek active Chinese cooperation. We recognize that a change in China's behavior is a prerequisite to getting a change in North Korea's behavior. And the President, the Secretary of State, and others have made crystal clear directly in private to Chinese leaders and in public that we think there is much more that China needs to do and can do and should do to tighten the screws on the DPRK, given their significant leverage and their special relationship.

Senator RUBIO. And all those moves are important, but we are talking about sanctions here. And yes, we sanctioned one company. There are multiple companies from China, China-related companies, who we have just as much evidence against. Everybody knows. I mean, everyone knows who they are. And when you look at how long it has taken to get to this point and you look at the limitations that have been placed where only one company has been designated so far when there are multiple companies of equal status and some actually are involved in even more of these sorts of deals, it starts to look like we are trying to not do too much too soon. And this notion of standard of proof—I understand about that if you are going to prosecute someone in Federal court, but from this perspective is a very different situation. This not even a secret. The world knows who these companies are.

And quite frankly, they do not necessarily take great steps to try to hide it on many occasions because the interest of the Chinese Government ultimately, beyond anything else, is stability in North Korea. They do not want to see a regime collapse and millions of people pouring over the border and in addition to a profit motive that is involved here as well for some of these companies. We know who these companies are. We have not moved fast enough on it. There is no reason not to have moved faster. There are plenty of targets of opportunity and plenty of information out there about them.

Senator GARDNER. And thank you, Senator Rubio. I would just remind Secretary Russel and the administration that under the sanctions act that we passed, these are mandatory investigations required and mandatory sanctions required unless the administration provides a waiver to Congress. At this point, do you intend to provide us with waivers of companies that you are investigating?

Ambassador FRIED. No.

Senator GARDNER. And so why have we only designated one company then?

Ambassador FRIED. As I said earlier, the Treasury Department, the State Department, and our intelligence community are all involved, engaged in investigations.

As Assistant Secretary Russel said, of course, the preferred option is for China itself to do more as we think it should.

A second option is to have Chinese companies independently come to the conclusion that it would be a lot better for them if they avoided interaction with North Korean companies.

But clearly our actions on Monday indicate that we are willing to sanction Chinese companies who are evading U.N. or U.S. sanctions. So we are pursuing all of these avenues.

Senator GARDNER. Senator Markey?

Senator MARKEY. Thank you, Mr. Chairman, very much.

We know that Kim Jong-un's goal is to die as a very old man in his bed. So that does not really work for him if there is an all-out nuclear war in that region because he would probably not become a very old man.

And so my concern here is the plans which are in place to use preemptive force against North Korea's nuclear arsenal or its leadership which could actually increase the risk of accidental nuclear war in a crisis.

Recently South Korea's Defense Minister informed the parliament that South Korea has forces on standby that are ready to assassinate Kim Jong-un if South Korea feels threatened by nuclear weapons. He said this. South Korea has a plan to use precision missile capabilities to target the enemy's facilities in major areas, as well as eliminating the enemy's leadership.

If North Korea fears that South Korea intends to use preemptive force to kill its leaders, then that could create huge pressures for Kim to delegate control over his nuclear weapons to frontline military commanders. And if North Korea believes that South Korea plans to preemptively take out its nuclear weapons, that could create pressure to use them or lose them in a crisis. Both of these pressures could drastically increase the risk of inadvertent nuclear war on the Peninsula.

Secretary Russel, in your view, is there a risk that military plans focused on preemptive attacks on North Korea's leadership and its nuclear arsenal could increase the risk of uncontrolled nuclear escalation? As part of your strategy for managing the North Korean nuclear threat, is the administration working on plans to deescalate a military crisis so that it does not spiral out of control and result in a nuclear war? And do you foresee potential arrangements for crisis communications with the North Korean regime to defuse and deescalate such a situation that could lead to an accidental nuclear war?

Mr. RUSSEL. The short answer, Senator Markey, is yes. We are concerned lest there be an escalatory cycle on the Korean Peninsula.

Yes, we have in place very serious counter-escalation plans in the U.S.-ROK alliance. The commander of the combined forces, General Vince Brooks, one of America's best soldiers, is, as his predecessors have been, working with the ROK military and national leadership on a day in and day out basis. They are very tightly stitched together.

And yes, the alliance has very specific plans to deal with a variety of contingencies with a view to, in the first instance, deescalating and defusing. This has been a big part of our joint defense strategy.

Now, there is a lot of hyperbole and rhetoric in the way that certainly North Korea speaks always and the way that some South Korean officials occasionally speak when they are out testifying or speaking before the press. I do not think that the comments of the defense minister, taken by themselves, represent an intent on the part of the Republic of Korea to take precipitant or provocative action.

Senator MARKEY. I appreciate that. My concern, obviously, is how the North Koreans react to it. Whether or not South Korea intends on doing it is separate from the paranoia that is induced in an individual or group of people that could then lead to an escalation. That is what we were always concerned about during the Cold War between the U.S. and USSR. It was an escalation of rhetoric that then could be used, unfortunately, by those that would think that nuclear weapons are usable. And so that is always a concern.

And what we are seeing actually following the 2013 North Korea nuclear test—a poll found that 66 percent of the South Korean public favored acquiring an independent nuclear deterrent.

After North Korea's test in January of this year, Won Yoo-chul, a senior South Korean figure in President Park's party, suggested that South Korea should acquire its own nuclear weapons. Referring to our nuclear umbrella that we provide, Won said, quote, we cannot borrow umbrellas from next door every time it rains. We should wear a raincoat of our own. We should get our own nuclear weapons.

How would you assess pressures in South Korean society to acquire nuclear weapons? How would you assess pressure inside of the Japanese society for them to acquire nuclear weapons? And what actions are we taking to reduce the likelihood that they move in that direction?

Mr. RUSSEL. Senator, I think that the pressure in the main stream political society in either the Republic of Korea or in Japan to contemplate the acquisition of nuclear weapons is directly commensurate with their faith in America's commitment as an ally to their defense and to the extended deterrence or the nuclear umbrella provided by their alliance with the United States.

Senator MARKEY. So you are saying they would have to believe that if there was, for example, a nuclear attack on South Korea, that we would then launch a nuclear attack on North Korea. They would have to believe that.

Mr. RUSSEL. I would put it the other way, Senator. If the Japanese and the Korean publics and their leaders lost faith in America's resolve, in our absolute determination to use all of these tools of national security to deter and to defend against an attack from North Korea, then yes, I think the——

Senator MARKEY. So how do you interpret this poll that says that 66 percent of the South Korean public favors acquiring an independent nuclear deterrent? Does that not indicate to you that there is some increasing lack of confidence in the American nuclear umbrella, that is, that we would actually use nuclear weapons against North Korea if there was such an attack or even a biological attack on South Korea?

Mr. RUSSEL. Well, I cannot speak to a particular poll. I think there is an ebb and flow among the Korean public. But certainly the concerns driven by North Korea's pattern of and tempo of testing is driving anxiety.

However, steps by the United States, such as the strong message of reaffirmation of our alliance commitments that President Obama made in his immediate phone calls to both President Park and to Prime Minister Abe, the deployment of our strategic bombers to the Korean Peninsula, the plans for bilateral and trilateral exercises, and the other manifestations of America's unshakeable determination to defend and protect ourselves and our allies, I believe keeps that kind of thinking——

Senator MARKEY. So you are saying that we are sending strong signals that you would use nuclear bombs on North Korea and that we are assuring the South Koreans that they do not have to have their own nuclear deterrent because we would use them in the event that there was a nuclear attack on South Korea. Is that what you are saying?

Mr. RUSSEL. No. Senator, what I am saying is that we are giving enough confidence to our allies——

Senator MARKEY. Confidence that what? That we would do what?

Mr. RUSSEL. That our deterrence——

Senator MARKEY. That our nuclear bombs——

Mr. RUSSEL.—and our willingness to utilize——

Senator MARKEY. To use them?

Mr. RUSSEL.—the full range of U.S.——

Senator MARKEY. Right. That is what I am saying. We are giving them confidence that we would use nuclear bombs against North Korea. Is that what you are saying?

Mr. RUSSEL. I am not going to say. I leave it to the President to decide if and when the United States is going to use a nuclear weapon. What I am saying is——

Senator MARKEY. But that is what I am hearing you say. Those are exactly the words that you are using. You are not saying "nuclear bomb" but you are using every other word but that to describe the use of a nuclear bomb.

Mr. RUSSEL. The way, Senator, that I think it should be understood is that the certainty on the part of the DPRK that the United States would either prevent their use of nuclear weapons or retaliate in a devastating manner is an effective deterrent, and the credibility of the U.S. deterrent is such that neither government intends to pursue nuclear weapons.

Senator MARKEY. I guess what I would say is we should really intensify our efforts to make sure that there is no accidental situation that develops that could increase tensions, that we are working very closely, that we are creating close communications with the North Korean Government in terms of the deployment of their weapons so that we do not have that accident and we do not have to ever have to use a nuclear weapon ourselves against the North Koreans because we do not know where that would end.

Thank you, Mr. Chairman, very much.

Senator GARDNER. Senator Udall?

Senator UDALL. Thank you, Mr. Chairman.

And thank you both for being here.

Retired Admiral Mullen and former Senator Sam Nunn recently made recommendations with regard to how to deal with the threat from North Korea. These included many recommendations for how to get North Korea back to the negotiating table. Has the State Department reviewed these recommendations, and do you believe that it is possible to restart negotiations?

Mr. RUSSEL. Thank you, Senator.

I recently sat down with both Admiral Mullen, with whom I had previously worked when he was Chairman and whom I deeply admire, and Senator Nunn to work through in some detail their recommendations in the report. I had been in touch with them during the process of writing the report, as well as with other important members of the committee. I think that we see things in a generally consistent manner.

The goal of U.S. policy has been to try engineer negotiations with North Korea over their nuclear program on the simple grounds that that is the only peaceful way forward to achieve denuclearization.

But the terms of those negotiations are very important. There is not only no value in talk for talk's sake, but the experience of the first Bush presidency, the Clinton presidency, the Bush 44 presidency, and our own experience has demonstrated that unless the negotiations are about North Korea's nuclear program and unless they include discussion of IAEA access and monitoring, North Korea simply cannot be trusted to honor its promises.

What the North Koreans have done is to, number one, abandon the Six Party Talks, renounce the commitments they have made under those talks, reject and defy international law in the form of the U.N. Security Council resolutions, and continue their violations while fitfully occasionally offering to hold discussions with the United States about the withdrawal of U.S. forces from South Korea. That is an utterly unacceptable basis for talks.

But we have worked consistently to show the North Koreans that we want to negotiate, that we are willing to talk, that the door is open to a process that can net them the benefits that were on the table in 2005 in the Six Party Talks process, which includes discussions about a successor agreement to an armistice, that includes the process of diplomatic normalization, economic assistance, and so on. And Secretary Kerry has gone out of his way both publicly but also in international meetings where the North Korean foreign minister was present to emphasize our interest and willingness to negotiate.

Senator UDALL. Do you have any additional comments on that?

Ambassador FRIED. No.

Senator UDALL. No.

How can we strengthen our monitoring capabilities to prevent North Korea from obtaining nuclear materials and equipment that it could use to create additional nuclear weapons? Does Congress need to invest more in technology and equipment to better monitor such transfers?

Ambassador FRIED. Senator, monitoring the materials that go into North Korea and that come out of North Korea, monitoring the movement of DPRK scientists and officials who might be involved in proliferation is a top priority for our national security agencies, as it is for those of Japan, Korea, and I believe China. We are working to share information. We are working to tighten the safeguards and the monitoring.

As for what additional funding, authorities, or Congress action would assist that effort, I would have to consult with my colleagues in other agencies and propose they respond in a classified setting.

Senator UDALL. Okay. Thank you very much.

Thank you, Mr. Chairman.

Senator GARDNER. Thank you, Senator Udall.

We will go to a second round of questioning. I will begin with Senator Menendez.

Senator MENENDEZ. Thank you, Mr. Chairman.

Ambassador Fried, I pride myself on my preparation for these hearings. So I went back to my office after your answer, and I looked at OFAC's statement of Monday. You said in response to my question, we just sanctioned a bank on Monday. Well, I read from OFAC's statement that they imposed sanctions on Dandong Hongxiang Industrial Development Company and four individuals.

Now, is that company a bank?

Ambassador FRIED. Sir, it is not a bank. It is a financial company that worked with a sanctioned North Korean bank.

Senator MENENDEZ. It is different than saying that you sanctioned a bank.

Ambassador FRIED. Yes, sir.

Senator MENENDEZ. You did not sanction a bank on Monday.

Ambassador FRIED. We sanctioned a Chinese financial corporation.

Senator MENENDEZ. All right. Well, that is different from a bank.

Ambassador FRIED. Yes, sir.

Senator MENENDEZ. Let me ask you this. How many banks—banks—has the administration sanctioned as it relates to North Korea?

Ambassador FRIED. Do you mean banks in general or Chinese banks?

Senator MENENDEZ. Let us talk about Chinese banks.

Ambassador FRIED. No Chinese banks.

Senator MENENDEZ. No Chinese banks.

Ambassador FRIED. Not in China.

We have designated a number of North Korean——

Senator MENENDEZ. That is my point. That was the point that I was trying to drive at earlier. You have sanctioned no Chinese banks at the end of the day, and they are probably the major financial institutions for North Korea.

What this company, as I understand, did was made purchases of sugar and fertilizer on behalf of a designated Korean bank. It is a trading company, not a financial company.

So when I take testimony as a member of this committee, I need to make sure that testimony is accurate because I make decisions based upon it. And I must say that the information you gave me is not accurate. This was not a bank. This is a trading company. And finally, I got the answer that I wanted to hear, which is what I knew, is that you sanctioned no Chinese banks as it relates to North Korea.

And it is our hesitancy to do so that takes away one of the major instruments possible to change Chinese thinking. I am all for persuasion, if you can achieve it, but when you cannot and North Korea continues to advance its nuclear program in a way that becomes more menacing in its miniaturization in its missile technology, I do not know at what point we are going to continue to think that we can stop them when in fact they are pretty well on their way, and we allow them to continue to do so, and we do not use some of the most significant tools that we have.

So I am disappointed that you did not give me the right information.

Now, one final question to you, Mr. Secretary. I think the chairman had a separate private panel that suggested that the Chinese have basically created a preference over stability in the Korean Peninsula versus the challenge of North Korea pursuing this nuclear power, nuclear weapons, and missile technology.

Now, I am never for nuclear proliferation. But do you agree that that is the view that China has?

Mr. RUSSEL. Senator, what I have heard Xi Jinping say repeatedly is that China's three noes are no war, no chaos, and no nuclear weapons on the Korean Peninsula. So I think they have multiple objectives that are in conflict with each other, and we see, in part depending on North Korean behavior, in part depending on the pressure or the persuasion from the United States, some ebbs and flows, some shifts in the Chinese from a bias towards maintaining civility and preventing——

Senator MENENDEZ. War and chaos are in my mind equally the same to some degree. When you have war, you generally have some degree of chaos. No nuclear weapons. Because there are some who suggest that if that is their dynamic, then allowing South Korea to pursue the possibility of nuclear weapons changes China dynamics as to how far it is willing to push North Korea.

Mr. RUSSEL. I think that the Chinese are very mindful of the risk that either South Korea or Japan might distance itself from the U.S. nuclear umbrella and pursue their own capabilities, and that I believe ought to motivate China to redouble its efforts to push back on the North Koreans. That is only one of many examples of why we believe it is so in the best interest of China to tighten up on the North, to expand their cooperation with us, and to really abandon an old pattern of tolerating a significant amount of provocative and dangerous behavior by the DPRK.

The greatest driver of instability in Northeast Asia is North Korea's nuclear and missile program, and the actions that the United States is taking and will take, hand in hand with our allies, that China opposes, which China perceives as somehow containing it, are all driven by the growing threat from the DPRK. Secretary Kerry has said again and again if that threat diminishes, if that threat is eliminated, the rationale for the United States to take a more robust military posture in Northeast Asia goes with it.

Senator MENENDEZ. Thank you, Mr. Chairman. Thanks for your courtesy.

Senator GARDNER. Thank you, Senator Menendez.

I want to follow up on Senator Menendez's question on this issue of banks. I believe in the testimony—I am trying to look into the testimony. Perhaps you can just refresh my memory. The statement was made that North Korea is exporting about a billion dollars' worth of coal to China that is benefiting the North Korean nuclear activity. Is that correct?

Ambassador FRIED. Yes, that is our belief.

Senator GARDNER. Okay. And so let us assume that $1 billion is coming from—give or take some, is coming into North Korea from China for the purchase of coal that is benefiting the nuclear program. I assume they are using Chinese banks—is that correct—for this coal and the importation and the payment of that coal?

Ambassador FRIED. The North Korean export of coal is certainly the largest single generator of foreign currency for the North Korean economy generally. It is a slightly different question as to whether that money directly funds its nuclear weapons and missile programs. However, for the purposes of our sanctions, that difference—and because money is fungible, that difference is not dispositive.

Senator GARDNER. And so are they using Chinese banks?

Ambassador FRIED. We are looking into exactly the mechanisms by which the coal goes from North Korea to China. I do not way to say specifically the role of banks versus the role of trading companies or other institutions. But we are looking hard and actively at the coal trade generally.

Senator GARDNER. So earlier in this conversation, I asked if we were actively investigating Chinese entities.

Ambassador FRIED. Yes.

Senator GARDNER. Okay. So we are actively investigating Chinese entities.

Ambassador FRIED. Yes.

Senator GARDNER. So we can expect and should expect sanctions to be issued against a number of Chinese entities. Is that correct? And if that is not correct, then when will the administration be sending waivers to Congress? And you said earlier that we do not anticipate waivers to be issued.

Ambassador FRIED. That is true.

Senator GARDNER. So when can we anticipate these additional sanctions to be made?

Ambassador FRIED. As my colleague and I said, the best option, the most effective way to put sustained and sustainable pressure on North Korea, which is our objective here, is to have China itself decide for its own purposes that this is where it wants to go.

A second way to proceed is to convince Chinese companies, including banks, that it would be in their best interest not to deal with sanctioned or sanctionable activities.

The option of directly sanctioning Chinese entities is available.

Senator GARDNER. And mandatory if they violate the terms of our legislation.

Ambassador FRIED. Well, that is right.

What we are looking at is the most effective means to achieve this end. Our purpose is to put pressure on North Korea. The purpose of sanctions is to support a policy. My colleagues has spoken to the policy. I am just the sanctions guy. The purpose of sanctions is pressure on North Korea. We want to find the best tactics to do that. We are looking at all of the tools. That includes sanctions. That includes high-level discussions with the Chinese.

I look forward to being in touch with you, sir, with your committee, about our thinking as this progresses. But I can tell you that this is not a "go through the motions" exercise. We are serious about this in general and specifically with respect to coal.

Senator GARDNER. Then let me ask you this next question. Has the administration designated any actors/entities in North Korea for their cyber actions, cyber attacks against the United States?

Ambassador FRIED. Not specifically for cyber. However, some of our designations are so broad, I suspect that they capture cyber actors.

Senator GARDNER. So do we plan to issue any cyber sanctions under the terms of section 209 of the legislation, the North Korea Sanctions Enhancement Act?

Mr. RUSSEL. Mr. Chairman, the administration did levy sanctions against a number of North Korean individuals and entities in the wake of the Sony hack under our own presidential executive order that preceded the adoption and the signing of the North Korea Sanctions Act. We have not yet developed a case under the law against North Korean cyber actors, but we are working towards that end. There is no question that North Korea's cyber activities, both those that emanate directly from North Korea and from servers in third countries, represent a serious threat to us and to others. We are on it.

Senator GARDNER. Because I mean, as reported this summer, North Korean hackers steal blueprints for U.S. fighter jets. Have they been sanctioned under the legislation—these actors?

Mr. RUSSEL. The intelligence and the law enforcement community in the U.S. Government is looking at and seeking to develop cases in order to sanction North Korean actors for any transgression.

Senator GARDNER. You talked a little bit about Air Koryo. Has the administration initiated investigations for designation of Air Koryo under the law, and does it believe it is engaged in activities that would make it eligible for designation?

Ambassador FRIED. In this setting, Mr. Chairman, I do not want to discuss specific investigations. It is true that we and our allies have curtailed Air Koryo's activities and restricted its ability—third governments have restricted its ability to land. I do not want to discuss in this session, in an open session, particular investigations, but we are well aware of Air Koryo's role in the North Korean system.

Senator GARDNER. Secretary Russel, we talked earlier in the hearing about United Nations Security Council Resolution 2270. Can you tell me a little bit more about China's implementation of 2270, particularly as it relates to coal? And Ambassador Fried maybe.

Mr. RUSSEL. Yes. I will make a general comment and then turn it over to Ambassador Fried.

The general comment is that I would characterize China's implementation of 2270 as incomplete, as a mixed bag. We have seen some clear indications that China has strengthened sanctions enforcement. That includes improved customs enforcement. The Chinese have publicly and privately asserted unequivocally that they consider themselves fully bound by the terms of 2270. But as I have said repeatedly and quoted President Obama and Secretary Kerry saying, we think that there is much more that they can do.

I have had quite a number of conversations with a variety of Chinese counterparts on this very subject both in China and elsewhere. They point out the not inconsiderable challenges that they face, given the extent of the Chinese-North Korean border and the degree of commerce and their concern about the livelihood and the welfare of North Korean people, so they say.

But right now, Mr. Chairman, I think our principal focus is the next generation of sanctions that we are seeking to obtain through a new U.N. Security Council resolution in New York, and that includes making some adjustments to provisions under 2270 to address some of the problems that you have flagged.

Senator GARDNER. And, Ambassador Fried, before you answer the question, I think in our briefing material given to every member of this committee it talked about China's announcement number 11, instructions to businesses on implementation of U.N. Security Council Resolution 2270. And it talked about the sample letter that an entity could provide to the government to basically claim the livelihood exemption, and it basically says my company is importing blank product. I hereby solemnly commit that this transaction is—with no documentation required.

So when it gets to the issue of the livelihood exemption, Ambassador Fried, the second United Nations Security Council resolution, what will it do to change China's behavior so that it can fully implement the sanctions and deprive the regime of foreign currency used to further develop its nuclear program?

Ambassador FRIED. Your question, Mr. Chairman, is the right one, but because this involves negotiations in the U.N. with the Chinese, I cannot predict where we will come out.

But I will say this. Security Council resolutions are the gold standard in sanctions because they are universal. They have unchallenged legitimacy and they are binding. But we are not bound by what the Security Council will accept. We have our national sanctions.

We would prefer to see an UNSCR address this issue. If not, we have options. And as I said earlier today, we are actively developing our options.

Senator GARDNER. And do those options involve actions at the United Nations? Are there other options, I mean, compliance mechanisms within the United Nations to enforce——

Ambassador FRIED. Certainly, sir. We work through the U.N. North Korea Sanctions Committee. We work with them on a regular basis. This spring I spent a day with them in a very detailed session with experts from Treasury, State Department, other agencies. So certainly we do that.

But we have to pursue all of the avenues.

Senator GARDNER. I want to get into some of those other avenues here in just a second. But does that committee have the ability to determine what nations are and are not fully enforcing 2270, and have they made that determination?

Ambassador FRIED. The Sanctions Committee does issue reports, and governments submit to that committee reports on their own implementation of 2270.

Senator GARDNER. And what is the finding of that report in regards to the country that is responsible for 90 percent of North Korea's economy?

Ambassador FRIED. I would say Assistant Secretary Russel summed that up pretty well: a mixed picture, although far better in action than before. There is a way to go.

Senator GARDNER. And so are there mechanisms within the United Nations to—compliance mechanisms—to enforce the resolution, and has the United States utilized those mechanisms and do we intend to?

Ambassador FRIED. We intend to use all avenues, including at the U.N., including the Sanctions Committee, to work to identify sanctionable activity to use this to improve everyone's enforcement—well, first, recognition of the provisions of 2270 and the enforcement of it. So certainly.

Senator GARDNER. And could you address some of the other options that you referred to in your answer?

Ambassador FRIED. Certainly.

What I said earlier about convincing Chinese companies that it is in their best interest to avoid sanctionable activity is not just a phrase. Our actions on Monday indicate that Chinese companies, you know, the financial company and the individuals, that Chinese persons fiscal, legal, and physical are not off limits. That news will spread around the Chinese community. We can also use various means to get the word out to Chinese businesses and banks that we are serious.

The Congress has given us and we have given ourselves under IEEPA wide authorities to act against sanctionable activity. The best sanctions are those that do not have to be used because the activity stops. The purpose of sanctions is not punish but to change behavior. If sanctions serve their purpose and behavior changes, to be specific, the exports of coal diminish because the costs and risks of doing so increase, so much the better. But the credibility of that kind of a message will grow as our determination becomes apparent.

When the Congress and the executive branch are pointed in the same direction, we are at our most powerful, which is why the legislation is so useful to us. We intend in the coming weeks and in the life of this administration to pursue all of these avenues with the objective of squeezing the North Korean economy in the service of the political objective that my colleague laid out.

Mr. RUSSEL. Mr. Chairman, if I could add, in addition to coal, North Korea has other revenue streams that we target. An important one is overseas labor, the export of workers both in restaurants and in forestry and agriculture, et cetera, which generates significant revenue for the country and for the regime.

We have under our executive orders the authority to target North Korea's export of labor on a unilateral basis, and we also have launched a worldwide effort to persuade recipient countries, contracting countries, and companies to end this practice and to forego the use of North Korean labor. We have had some successes. The media has also covered the defection of some of the North Korean restaurant workers, which has forced the North Koreans to double down on their security restrictions and limit themselves in who they send and how many they send. This is another area where we are continuing to work to close off a revenue stream.

Senator GARDNER. And what more can be done on the human trafficking, labor trafficking front? I think that is a very serious issue that a number of countries are involved in perhaps unwittingly but most likely knowingly.

Mr. RUSSEL. Oh, yes.

Senator GARDNER. What more can the United States do? And do you have all the authorities that we need through U.N. as well as U.S. law to intercede?

Ambassador FRIED. Senator, a number of companies are sensitive to this issue and when a light is shined on it, they have reacted well. So we, State Department and Treasury colleagues, have been going around to third country governments. We are working with third governments about this. We also intend to pursue this with the Chinese and the Russians because they are significant importers of North Korean labor. So we are prepared to advance this issue just as my colleague said.

We have the authorities we need, but since, Mr. Chairman, you asked, it would be useful I think if you were sending similar messages, and we are happy to stay in touch about this.

Senator GARDNER. Sending messages to——

Ambassador FRIED. Third countries.

Senator GARDNER.——third countries about their—I think we have made it very clear through our actions on this committee that we condemn any such activity, particularly the access or the abuse that those workers encounter abroad, as well as the contribution that they are again unintentionally providing to the North Korean regime and its ballistic missile program through work abroad, two-thirds of their wages then or more being utilized by the Government of North Korea.

Ambassador FRIED. I could not agree more, sir. And it is, as I said, enormously helpful when the executive branch and the Congress are pointed in the same direction.

Senator GARDNER. Do you believe you need additional authorities?

Ambassador FRIED. I do not think we need additional authorities. We need to continue work with potentially cooperative third governments, and that is what we are doing. And we are working, of course, closely with the Japanese and South Koreans to approach other governments. And we are working through the issue of Chinese and Russian imports of labor, particularly Chinese.

Senator GARDNER. So China and Russia. What other allies, though, do we have a close working relationship that need to hear that message from Congress?

Ambassador FRIED. Well, there are governments in the Middle East and a couple in Europe, but some of them have started taking action already, partly because they were responsive to our concerns and I believe yours.

Senator GARDNER. The issue of labor—has it extended into other—restaurants you talked about. Has it extended into other fields that perhaps we are worried about from other considerations?

Ambassador FRIED. We believe so. We are looking into the details of the use of North Korean labor. Some of this is classified, and I am happy to discuss it in another setting. But as we discover in specific information, we may have opportunities to approach both governments and companies.

Senator GARDNER. Thank you.

Could you elaborate further a little bit on any ongoing or previous cooperation between North Korea and Iran in their ballistic missile programs?

Mr. RUSSEL. Well, Mr. Chairman, we monitor and review all information, open source and intelligence information, on potential WMD activities and cooperation by both North Korea and Iran and definitely any potential nexus whereby either would seek to acquire proliferation-sensitive information or materials from the others.

As you know well, the U.N. Security Council Resolution 2231 prohibits the sale or transfer to or from Iran of ballistic missiles and related items. We have unilateral and other multilateral sanctions against that.

So please rest assured that this is a focus of intense scrutiny on the part of U.S. national security agencies.

Senator GARDNER. So at this point, we do not believe there is any cooperation between Iran and North Korea on their ballistic missile program.

Mr. RUSSEL. Mr. Chairman, I think any deeper dive into this question should be done in a classified setting. But I myself am not aware of any evidence of cooperation currently on nuclear or missile programs.

Senator GARDNER. Ambassador Fried, do you wish to answer that?

Ambassador FRIED. A closed session would be a better place to discuss the past relationship between North Korea and Iran and our current projections.

Senator GARDNER. The new government in Burma, the cooperation between possible North Korean activities, the new government in Burma—how has that changed?

Mr. RUSSEL. There is not a change in terms of cooperation with the government of Burma on DPRK dealings, or to the extent that there is a change, it is for the better.

The problem continues to be the gap between the government and the Burmese military, and for that reason when the de facto leader of Burma, or Myanmar, Aung San Suu Kyi, was in Washington just 2 weeks ago, the U.S. senior officials, including the President, underscored the importance of her and the duly elected civilian government working with the Burmese military to root out and to stop any vestiges of cooperation that may have remained.

We also talked directly to the Burmese military leadership about the DPRK. I myself have met with the commander-in-chief during my visits to Burma, as have several of my colleagues, and our talented Ambassador, Scot Marciel, has met with him as well. We think that there are potentially a few residual pockets within the Burmese military of people who might still have some ongoing interactions, but we are——

Senator GARDNER. Ongoing interactions with?

Mr. RUSSEL. With DPRK that are, in effect, leftovers from 5-plus years ago, the era of the military dictatorship. But we think that as far as the government is concerned and the military leadership is concerned that they are fully onboard, and this is something that they are working to prevent and eradicate.

Senator GARDNER. I know that the conversations that we have had, though, with Burma recently, of course, talk about lifting of sanctions, the U.S. lifting of sanctions. Now, if they are still interacting or doing business with North Korea, that would be a violation of these sanctions.

Mr. RUSSEL. Right. Any actor in Burma found to be doing business with the North Korean military would be in violation both of our executive orders and legislation and of the U.N. Security Council resolutions and would be subject to sanctions. I believe that the government and the military leadership in Burma is firmly opposed to any of that activity and is actively seeking to ascertain whether any continues and, if so, to stop it.

Senator GARDNER. Thank you.

I want to stick with the subject of Burma here as we close out the hearing.

As you will recall, Secretary Russel, during the confirmation of Ambassador Marciel that you just mentioned to be Ambassador to Burma, I asked and received a letter from the State Department. The letter from the State Department stated that—and I quote— the Department is committed to full, robust, and timely consultation with you and your staff regarding U.S. policy toward Burma in general and sanctions policy in particular.

On September 14th, while Burma leader Aung San Suu Kyi was visiting Washington, President Obama announced that he will terminate the national emergency with regard to Burma and lift the remaining U.S. sanctions on the country. It was claimed this action was closely coordinated with Aung San Suu Kyi and approved by her as well.

Can you describe the time frame, the extent of the congressional consultation with regard to lifting those sanctions on Burma?

Mr. RUSSEL. My deputy and my staff, Mr. Chairman, including during the period where I was traveling overseas, met with members of the committee staff and other Senate and House staff to describe the trend line in our thinking in the run-up to Aung San Suu Kyi's visit.

The actual decision by the President to lift the state of national emergency, the IEEPA sanctions on Burma, was made within a day or a couple of days of the arrival of Aung San Suu Kyi. And it was subject to confirmation that that indeed was her request.

A couple of days or maybe a day or so—as soon as I learned about this, you will recall, I put in a phone call to you personally, in an effort to fulfill both that obligation but also in light of the good cooperation that we have had, to let you know where it was heading.

And the morning of Aung San Suu Kyi's meeting with President Obama, she attended a breakfast meeting hosted by Vice President Biden; with Senator Corker, the chairman of the full committee; and the Senate Majority Leader, Leader McConnell; and other members in which they asked her very directly if she wanted the sanctions lifted, and she said yes. So on that basis, in the subsequent meeting in the Oval Office, President Obama announced, after confirming it with her personally, to the press his intention to lift sanctions.

Senator GARDNER. Do you feel the State Department met the full, robust, and timely standard pledged to this committee?

Mr. RUSSEL. Well, Mr. Chairman, what really matters is whether you feel it, and if you do not, I will promise to do better. But it is my firm intent and desire to be responsive and open in sharing with you our policy, our thinking, and to ensure that there is an opportunity to consult with you and to take your views into account.

Senator GARDNER. Well, I do not think breakfast and a phone call are full, robust, and timely.

Do you support retaining sanctions on Burma military-controlled entities MEC and MEHL, which Aung San Suu Kyi herself said she supports?

Mr. RUSSEL. What I heard her say, Mr. Chairman, is that the time has come to lift all the sanctions and for the United States not to serve as a prop for Burma, but to be a supporter of the civilian government's exercise of authority over the military. So what we seek to do is to ensure that our programs and policies reinforce the restrictions on investment and on business, the controls and the regulations pertaining to business activities by the military and by MEC and MEHL specifically, that the Burmese Government chooses to put in place.

Senator GARDNER. Let me just cut through that. So you support continuing the sanctions on these military-controlled entities.

Mr. RUSSEL. No. I support finding practical ways that we can continue to discourage irresponsible investment and business activities with entities like MEC and MEHL, but to do so in support of the Government of Burma's own policies. And they are in the process now of making decisions in that regard.

Senator GARDNER. Thank you very much, Ambassador Fried, Secretary Russel. I appreciate your time today, with the thanks of the committee, providing us testimony and responses today.

Information for the members. The record will remain open until the close of business this Friday, September 30th, including for members to submit questions for the record. We ask the witnesses to respond as promptly as possible. Your responses will also be made part of the record.

I thank you very much for your service and thank you for the opportunity to be before the committee today. Thank you.

[Whereupon, at 11:59 a.m., the hearing was adjourned.]

---

## ADDITIONAL MATERIAL SUBMITTED FOR THE RECORD

### STATEMENT SUBMITTED BY SENATOR BARBARA BOXER

Mr. Chairman, Ranking Member Cardin, thank you for convening this important hearing today on North Korea.

Few issues pose as immediate a threat to the United States, and international stability, as North Korea's nuclear program. This will, without question, be one of the most pressing issues facing the next U.S. president.

One that will not—as some have recklessly suggested—be solved by encouraging Japan and South Korea to develop their own nuclear arsenals and triggering a catastrophic arms race in the region.

Although the North Korean regime has continued its dangerous and provocative behavior, I do commend President Obama for putting in place such a stringent regime of sanctions. I hope we, the Senate, can continue to work with the President on these efforts.

However, North Korea's escalating nuclear and ballistic missile tests demonstrate that we need to do much more to contain and halt the activities of this oppressive regime.

I look forward to hearing from our witnesses today on our best options, moving forward, to dismantle North Korea's nuclear program.

---

### RESPONSES TO QUESTIONS FOR THE RECORD SUBMITTED TO AMBASSADOR FRIED BY SENATOR RUBIO

*Question 1.* Even in this time of the failed JCPOA, there are three times as many Iran-related persons designated by the United States than North Korea-related persons, can you describe the reason for this discrepancy? When are we going to get into the regular habit of sanctioning North Korea-related persons and move beyond the provocation-response cycle?

*Answer.* Since 2010, we have been steadily ramping up the pressure on North Korea. There are five executive orders that impose sanctions specifically against North Korea. There are also other executive orders that are not specific to North Korea, but have been used to impose sanctions in connection with our twin goals of obstructing the nuclear program and bringing North Korea back to the negotiating table.

The administration intends to continue to move forward with new sanctions against North Korea as part of our comprehensive effort to address the country's malign behavior and obstruct its nuclear proliferation activities, independent of a provocation-response cycle. As of early November, the administration had issued four rounds of sanctions rollouts, Executive Order 13722, as well as other restrictive measures this year. These designations are the basis of our continued efforts to build pressure against North Korea in a consistent way, without being limited to a provocation-response cycle, and they follow four tranches of new sanctions designations rolled out in 2015.

North Korea poses particular challenges from a sanctions perspective, given its relative economic isolation and given that the regime prides itself on an ideology that values self-reliance above all. North Korea is a pariah state with a population of 25 million and a GDP of just $28 billion and therefore, it presents a more limited number of potential targets and opportunities to gather information about potentially sanctionable activities. Despite these challenges, we believe that viable targets can be identified will continue to look for opportunities to use economic and financial sanctions to compel the Kim regime to change its course.

*Question 2.* The conclusions in a recent study by the Center for Advanced Defense Studies and the Asan Institute for Policy Studies called "In China's Shadow," are concerning and encapsulate this administration's failed policy of "strategic patience." It is clear that China has allowed a Chinese company and its front company to conduct $532 million in trade volume. I want to ask a few questions about this activity. I am assuming that we were aware of these activities before they were exposed by these organizations, so why did we wait so long to act against these persons given the timeline of activities in the report date back to January 2011?

Answer. North Korea's economy indeed is heavily dependent on China. The administration has engaged Beijing at the highest levels to seek greater Chinese cooperation on imposing costs on North Korea for its threatening behavior. We regularly urge China to do more to prevent North Korea from using Chinese companies or infrastructure in ways that can benefit the DPRK's illicit activities. In addition, the administration uses other tools, including restrictive measures like sanctions, export controls, and criminal charges to increase the pressure on the DPRK and those aiding it in its illicit and dangerous activities.

We have seen the report by Asan Institute and the Center for Advanced Defense Studies (C4ADS), which shines light on North Korea's networks overseas. In addition to the DHID-related designations, State and Treasury have also taken steps to curb North Korea's shipping operations. Specifically, Treasury designated Ocean Maritime Management (OMM) and several of its front companies; OMM is highlighted in the Asan-C4ADS report as being a key conduit of North Korean overseas activity. The administration has also identified and blocked 18 vessels connected to OMM, while the Department of State has led diplomatic efforts to ensure the implementation of UN obligations on Member States related to prohibitions on flagging, owning, and operating DPRK-affiliated vessels.

*Question 3.* U.S. designated Ma Xiaohong is the chairwoman of the Liaoning Hongxiang Group, which is made up of six companies: U.S. designated Dandong Hongziang Industrial Development Co. Ltd. (DHID), Hongxiang International Freight, Liaoning Hongxiang International Travel Service Co Ltd., Dandong Hongxiang Border and Trade Consultant Service Co., Qibaoshan (Chilbosan) Hotel, and Pyongyang (Liujing) Restaurant.

- ♦ Have you initiated an investigation of Hongxiang International Freight, Liaoning Hongxiang International Travel Service Co Ltd., Dandong Hongxiang Border and Trade Consultant Service Co., Qibaoshan (Chilbosan) Hotel, and Pyongyang (Liujing) Restaurant as required by Section 102 of the North Korea Sanctions and Policy Enhancement Act of 2016 (P.L. 114–122)?

- ♦ If so, why have these companies not been designated as required by the mandatory sanctions in P.L. 114–122?

- ♦ If not, why?

Answer. On September 26, 2016, the Treasury Department and the Justice Department moved in concert to investigate the sanctions evasion activities undertaken by a Chinese entity and four Chinese nationals: Dandong Hongxiang Industrial Development Company Ltd (DHID), Ma Xiaohong, Zhou Jianshu, Hong Jinhua, and Luo Chuanxu. The Treasury Department added these persons to OFAC's List of Specially Designated Nationals and Blocked Persons, while the Justice Department unsealed criminal charges against the same for conspiring to evade U.S. economic sanctions and launder money, and violating OFAC's Weapons of Mass Destruction Proliferators Sanctions Regulations. We have not shied away from imposing sanctions on third-country actors, nor do we intend to.

The sanctions applied to date have created significant problems for the North Korean regime, but they have not yet caused the DPRK to change course. The administration is in close coordination with our allies and key partners, especially Japan and South Korea, and including China as well, and is continually examining our sanctions toolkit and identifying ways to improve its efficacy and increase pressure on the DPRK.

Consistent with the North Korea Sanctions and Policy Enhancement Act, and as a priority matter of sanctions implementation, the Treasury Department and other parts of the interagency continue to look for credible, well-sourced, and recent evidence to support future designations and diplomatic actions—including those involving third-country parties. We would be happy discuss the specifics of these matters in a classified, interagency briefing.

*Question 4.* In the report referenced in question #2, the "Chilbosan Hotel in Shenyang, one of Liaoning Hongziang's joint ventures with the DPRK, is alleged to be the staging area for Bureau 121, a group of North Korean hackers. It has been widely reported that Bureau 121 may have been responsible for the 2014 Sony hack"

- ♦ In an additional question to question #3, does the investigation of Chilbosan Hotel include its links to DPRK cyber activities as required by Section 104 of the North Korea Sanctions and Policy Enhancement Act of 2016 (P.L. 114–122)

Answer. Consistent with the North Korea Sanctions and Policy Enhancement Act, and as a consistent matter of sanctions maintenance, the Treasury Department and other parts of the interagency continue to look for credible and well-sourced evidence to support future designations and diplomatic actions—including those involving third-country parties. We would be happy to discuss the specifics of these matters in a classified, interagency briefing.

*Question 5.* (Pg 33.) In the report referenced in question #2 Liaoning Hongbao Industrial Development Co. Ltd. is a joint venture between U.S.-designated Dandong Hongziang Industrial Development Co. Ltd. (DHID) and Korea National Insurance Corporation (KNIC), the German branch of KNIC was designated by the EU.

- ♦ Have you initiated an investigation of Liaoning Hongbao Industrial Development Co. Ltd.as required by Section 102 of the North Korea Sanctions and Policy Enhancement Act of 2016 (P.L. 114–122)?
- ♦ If so, why have these companies not been designated as required by the mandatory sanctions in P.L. 114–122?
- ♦ If not, why?

Answer. Consistent with the North Korea Sanctions and Policy Enhancement Act, and as a consistent matter of sanctions maintenance, the Treasury Department and other parts of the interagency continue to look for credible and well-sourced evidence to support future designations and diplomatic actions—including those involving third-country parties. We would be happy to discuss the specifics of these matters in a classified, interagency briefing.

*Question 6.* Please provide a reason why the Obama administration has not provided a waiver of the requirement to impose sanctions under the North Korea Sanctions and Policy Enhancement Act of 2016 (P.L. 114–122) for the following entities:

- ♦ Dandong Hongxiang Border and Trade Consultant Service Co.
- ♦ Liaoning Hongxiang International Travel Service Co. Ltd.
- ♦ Hongxiang International Freight
- ♦ Chilbosan Hotel
- ♦ Liujing Restaurant
- ♦ Liaoning Hongbao Industrial Development Co. Ltd.

Answer. The administration has vigorously and faithfully implemented the North Korea Sanctions and Policy Enhancement Act (NKSPEA) in all matters, including with regard to the entities listed above. A few examples of the administration's efforts include:

- *June 9, 2016:* The State Department transmitted a NKSPEA-mandated Report to Congress on actions taken to implement the U.S. strategy to improve international implementation of UN sanctions on North Korea.
- *June 30, 2016:* The Treasury Department, with support from the State Department and the Office of the Director of National Intelligence, submitted a NKSPEA-mandated report to Congress on North Korea's activities undermining cybersecurity, as one of a number of reports mandated by the Act. In the report, the State Department outlines the U.S. government's strategy to engage foreign partners to combat such activity.
- *July 6, 2016:* The State Department published the NKSPEA-mandated Report to Congress on human rights abuses in North Korea. Based in part on information contained in the report, the Treasury Department makes 16 additions to the SDN list, including Kim Jong Un.
- *August 11, 2016:* The State Department transmitted a NKSPEA-mandated Report to Congress on U.S. policy toward North Korea based on a complete interagency review of policy alternatives.

- *August 24, 2016:* The State Department transmitted a NKSPEA-mandated Report to Congress regarding the U.S. strategy to promote initiatives to enhance international awareness and address the human rights situation in North Korea.
- *September 1, 2016:* The State Department transmitted a NKSPEA-mandated Report to Congress detailing a plan for making unrestricted, unmonitored, and inexpensive mass communication available to the people of North Korea.
- *September 26, 2016:* The Treasury Department designated four Chinese nationals and one entity complicit in sanctions evasion activities, consistent with mandatory sanctions in the Act.

We would be happy to discuss the activities of the above-mentioned entities in a classified, interagency briefing.

*Question 7.* The Department of Justice unsealed indictments and a civil forfeiture action related to these transactions. The criminal indictment lists transactions in millions of U.S. dollars going back to 2009 where these front companies "served as financial intermediaries for U.S. dollar transactions between North Korean-based entities who were being financed by KKBC [a designated North Korean bank] and suppliers in other countries in order to evade the restrictions on U.S. dollar transactions," why did we wait to act against these persons? Will you state for the record that the White House or State Department did not pressure the Justice Department or Treasury Department to delay these designations and law enforcement actions to avoid embarrassing China?

Answer. As a matter of policy, the State Department does not interfere in matters of law enforcement. We refer you to the Department of Justice for more information on the evolution of the criminal case involving sanctions evasion in support of KKBC.

*Question 8.* I would like to turn to the decision by the Treasury Department in June to finally designate the jurisdiction of North Korea as a primary money laundering concern, an action that only occurred after Congress passed the North Korea Sanctions Enforcement Act of 2016. In the notice of finding, it stated that "In 2013, senior North Korean leadership utilized a KKBC front company to open accounts at a major Chinese bank under the names of Chinese citizens, and deposited millions of U.S. dollars into the accounts. The same KKBC front company processed transactions through U.S. correspondent accounts as recently as 2013." Are these the same persons in this week's actions? If so, why did we wait several months after the June Treasury action before addressing this illicit use of the U.S. financial system? The same finding stated that another designated North Korean bank used a front company to process financial transactions through the U.S. financial system more than a year after its designation, again why did we wait so long to address these activities?

Answer. The Treasury Department finalized its Section 311 rulemaking with respect to North Korea on November 4, 2016. We believe that the Section 311 final rule regarding North Korea was an important step in further isolating North Korea from the international financial system. In addition to being consistent with the North Korea Sanctions and Policy Enhancement Act, it also amplifies the sanctions imposed by United Nations Security Council Resolution (UNSCR) 2270, which was unanimously adopted on March 2, 2016. Among other significant restrictions, UNSCR 2270 requires Member States to sever correspondent banking relationships with North Korean financial institutions by May 31, 2016 (90 days).

––––––––

RESPONSES TO QUESTIONS FOR THE RECORD SUBMITTED
TO AMBASSADOR FRIED BY SENATOR GARDNER

*Question 1.* On March 18, 2016, New York Times reported they uncovered documents, which showed how a ZTE, a Chinese firm, "would set up seemingly independent companies—called 'cut-off companies'—that would sign the deals in other countries. That could enable it to continue to do business in Iran, North Korea and other countries placed under American restrictions."

On June 2, 2016, New York Times reported that the U.S. Commerce Department is also investigating the Chinese company Huawei, including demanding that the company "turn over all information regarding the export or re-export of American technology to Cuba, Iran, North Korea, Sudan and Syria, according to a subpoena sent to Huawei and viewed by The New York Times. The subpoena is part of an investigation into whether Huawei broke United States export controls."

♦ What are ZTE and Huawei's dealings with North Korea?

♦ Are North Korean nationals, or individuals working at the behest of the North Korean regime, utilizing any Huawei or ZTE equipment to conduct cyberattacks?

Answer. We do not comment on ongoing investigations. Generally speaking, the recent Executive Order signed by President Obama (EO 13722) imposed prohibitions on the exportation from the U.S. or the re-exportation from abroad of goods, services, and technology to North Korean entities, except where licensed by the Commerce or Treasury Department, as appropriate. In addition, Commerce has long required licenses for all exports and reexports, except for food and medicine, to North Korea. We refer you to the Treasury and Commerce Departments for more information about their efforts.

EO 13722 also authorizes new sanctions designations for those engaging in significant activities undermining cybersecurity against targets outside of North Korea on behalf of the Government North Korea or the Workers' Party of Korea. This includes the ability to impose sanctions on persons providing material assistance, sponsorship, or financial, material, or technological support for, or goods and services to or in support of any person undermining or attempting to undermine cybersecurity on behalf of the Government of North Korea or the Korean Workers Party. This authority is consistent with those outlined in the North Korea Sanctions Policy Enhancement Act.

Dealings with North Korea by ZTE and Huawei is a topic that would be best addressed via an interagency briefing in a classified setting after the investigation has concluded.

*Question 2.* If there is evidence that ZTE or Huawei have collaborated with the North Korean regime to conduct illicit activities, would you support their designation under the North Korea Sanctions and Policy Enhancement Act or any other legal authorities?

Answer. We do not comment on ongoing investigations. We have used our sanctions authorities and other restrictive measures against third-country nationals and entities, including Chinese. For example, on September 26, 2016, the Treasury Department imposed sanctions on four Chinese nationals and one Chinese entity that were found to be supporting North Korea's WMD proliferation activities.

We will continue to use all tools at our disposal in order to halt North Korea's nuclear proliferation activities, deprive the Kim regime of hard currency, and protect the United States from threats to our national security.

-------

RESPONSES TO QUESTIONS FOR THE RECORD SUBMITTED
TO AMBASSADOR FRIED BY SENATOR PERDUE

*Question 1.* The importance of China's role in enforcement of these sanctions cannot be overstated. Between 2011 and 2015, more than 90% of North Korea's trade with the outside world is believed to have been with China and South Korea. Can you describe the administration's current efforts to influence China to leverage its relationship with North Korea (DPRK) to fully implement sanctions?

Answer. The administration has engaged Beijing at the highest levels to seek greater Chinese cooperation in imposing costs on North Korea for its threatening behavior. We regularly urge China to do more to prevent North Korea from using Chinese companies or infrastructure in ways that can benefit the DPRK's illicit activities. All options, including sanctions, remain on the table. We are not shying away from their use.

On September 26, the Treasury Department and the Justice Department moved in concert to check the sanctions evasion activities undertaken by a Chinese entity and four Chinese nationals: Dandong Hongxiang Industrial Development Company Ltd (DHID), Ma Xiaohong, Zhou Jianshu, Hong Jinhua, and Luo Chuanxu. The Treasury Department added these persons to the Specially Designated Nationals List, while the Justice Department unsealed criminal charges against the same for conspiring to evade U.S. economic sanctions and violating OFAC's Weapons of Mass Destruction Proliferators Sanctions Regulations as well as conspiracy to launder money.

We will continue to urge China to exert its leverage as North Korea's largest trading partner. We seek to force Kim Jong Un come to the realization that the only viable path forward for his country is denuclearization.

*Question 2.* The U.N. Sanctions Committee has difficulty with collecting the data necessary to properly enforce sanctions against North Korea. A major reason analysts give for this is that it is broadly suspected that China's border with North Korea is significantly porous, allowing any flow of goods between the two countries to go undocumented. Is the administration looking into ways to influence China to a) fully comply with reporting requirements under DPRK sanctions, and b) to begin to enforce their border with North Korea more stringently?

Answer. We agree that more work is needed to limit the flow of illicit goods over the China-North Korea border and we continue to work closely with the Chinese to achieve greater cooperation and application of pressure on North Korea. While we are aware of China's concerns that pressure on North Korea could precipitate a destabilizing crisis, we consider North Korea's nuclear and missile programs as posing a far greater threat to regional security. We acknowledge steps China has taken to implement U.N. sanctions but have repeatedly urged China to improve its implementation and apply pressure needed to effect a change in North Korea's behavior.

China has objected to U.S. actions intended to strengthen our defenses against North Korean military threats to ourselves and our allies, but we have made clear that we will take all necessary steps to deter and defend against those threats. We closely coordinate with China on sanctions and other measures to counter North Korea's problematic behavior.

*Question 3.* We also know that U.N. sanctions have, in some ways, had the perverse effect of actually boosting revenue flows to North Korea. Due to certain sanctions exemptions, such as those allowing the importation of goods from North Korea when the profits from such imports are generated "for the people's livelihood," trade with China and South Korea has increased by 90% in 2011. Further, China has exploited these exemptions to increase their North Korean imports of irons and iron ore by 64 percent. However, certification that these imports comply with sanctions exemptions are enforced by China's own custom's authorities, creating a significant conflict of interest.

- How has the administration gone about addressing the issue of exemptions with China?

- Has the administration discussed the possibility of defining "for the people's livelihood" exemption with the Sanctions Committee or with China? If so, how?

- Alternatively, has the administration sought to persuade China to raise the bar for businesses seeking to take advantage of the "livelihoods" exception by requiring some type of documentation? If so, what kind? Would there be any possibility of an oversight mechanism outside of Chinese customs authorities?

Answer. The administration is deeply troubled by the increase in the exports of North Korean coal to China, including under the "livelihood" exception. Not only is North Korean coal in many cases mined by essentially enslaved workers—including children—it helps to prop up the Kim regime at the expense of everyday North Koreans, making coal harder to obtain for those seeking to heat their homes and cook their food.

We are taking immediate steps to address this problem. Specifically, the U.S. Mission to the United Nations in New York is seeking ways to limit DPRK exports of coal that benefit the regime. If those efforts fail to produce the desired narrowing of the UNSCR 2270 livelihoods exception, the administration stands ready to continue high-level diplomatic engagement with all importers of North Korean coal, iron and iron ore, and consider the best way to promote stronger and global implementation of UNSCR 2270, potentially including by using domestic sanctions authorities.

*Question 4.* A key question for implementation of sanctions continues to be whether China will inspect shipments on its border, through its ports, and in its air space, for shipments of illicit goods and materials to and from North Korea. China is not a participant in the Proliferation Security Initiative (PSI), which holds regular information-sharing and ship-boarding exercises to improve international coordination and facilitate timely interdictions. Has the administration explored increasing cooperation with other PSI countries, namely at key transshipment points, to improve intelligence collection and information sharing on illicit shipments to and from North Korea?

Answer. North Korea's economy is indeed heavily dependent on China. The administration has engaged Beijing at the highest levels to seek greater Chinese cooperation on imposing costs on North Korea for its threatening behavior. We regularly urge China to do more to prevent North Korea from using Chinese companies or infrastructure in ways that can benefit the DPRK's illicit activities. At times, the administration turns to other tools, including restrictive measures like sanctions, export controls, and criminal proceedings.

We have seen the report by Asan Institute and C4ADS, which shines light on North Korea's overseas networks. In addition to the recent DHID-related designations, State and Treasury have also taken steps to curb North Korea's shipping operations. Specifically, Treasury designated Ocean Maritime Management (OMM) and several of its front companies; OMM is highlighted in a recent report by the Asan Institute and C4ADS as being a key conduit of North Korean overseas activity. The administration has also identified as blocked 18 vessels connected to OMM.

Furthermore, the administration secured the listing of 31 vessels controlled or operated by OMM in UNSCR 2270, along with many new maritime sanctions authorities that better enable a global campaign to shut down North Korea's maritime activities. The administration is also seeking to further strengthen U.N. sanctions in this realm. The Department of State has led diplomatic efforts to ensure the implementation of U.N. obligations on Member States related to prohibitions on flagging, owning, and operating DPRK-affiliated vessels.

PSI partners in the region have hosted several bilateral and multilateral events, workshops, and exercises. In September 2016, the third annual PSI Asia-Pacific Exercise Rotation (PSI-APER) event was held in Singapore, which included an at-sea live boarding exercise, an in-port interdiction demonstration, and a tabletop exercise and policy discussion. A key focus of the tabletop exercise was on the importance of timely and accurate intelligence and information to fulfill commitments that countries make when they endorse the PSI Statement of Interdiction Principles. These commitments include undertaking "effective measures, either alone or in concert with other states, for interdicting the transfer or transport of WMD, their delivery systems, and related materials to and from states and non-state actors of proliferation concern." Australia will host the next PSI APER event in 2017.

*Question 5.* Why has Treasury not yet cut off North Korea, financial institutions that facilitate transactions for the government, as well as third parties that use those institutions, from any access to the U.S. financial system? In June of this year, the Treasury Department announced its finding that DPRK is a jurisdiction of primary money laundering concern. At the same time, Treasury also released a notice of proposed rulemaking recommending a special measure to prohibit covered U.S. financial institutions from opening or maintaining correspondent accounts with North Korea financial institutions, and prohibiting the use of U.S. correspondent accounts to process transactions for North Korean institutions.

♦ What is keeping Treasury from implementing this rule?

♦ What steps is the administration taking to educate U.S. financial institutions about this new policy?

♦ Has Treasury considered also targeting third-party banks that use those financial messaging services?

Answer. We believe that the Section 311 final rule regarding North Korea will be an important step in further isolating North Korea from the international financial system, despite the fact that it was already one of the most heavily sanctioned countries. In addition to being consistent with the North Korea Sanctions and Policy Enhancement Act, it would also amplify the sanctions imposed by United Nations Security Council Resolution (UNSCR) 2270, which was passed on March 2, 2016. Among other significant restrictions, UNSCR 2270 requires Member States to sever correspondent banking relationships with North Korean financial institutions by May 31, 2016.

While North Korea's financial institutions do not maintain correspondent accounts with U.S. financial institutions, the North Korean government continues to use state-controlled financial institutions and front companies to surreptitiously conduct illicit international financial transactions, some of which support the proliferation of weapons of mass destruction and the development of ballistic missiles. While current U.S. law already generally prohibits U.S. financial institutions from engaging in both direct and indirect transactions with North Korean financial institutions, we anticipate that the final rule under Section 311 will support international sanctions already in place against North Korea and provide greater protection for the U.S. financial system from North Korean illicit activity.

While we cannot comment publicly on future sanctions actions, we can assure you that we will continue working with our international partners to cut off services to North Korea's banking sector.

*Question 6.* After DPRK conducted its 5th nuclear test, the U.S. flew several B1 stealth bombers over South Korea as a showcase of our military force. In your opinion, have these flights had an effect in North Korea's decision-making?

Answer. Yes. The B1 bomber flights had two purposes. First, to deter DPRK aggression and second, to assure the ROK public. The two separate B1 flights in September demonstrated both the regular availability and rapid responsiveness of U.S. strategic capabilities and was intened to deter DPRK aggression against the ROK and Japan. The U.S. ability to project power onto the Korean Peninsula was a signal that was heavily publicized and successfully communicated to the DPRK through USG press releases. These flights were also designed to assure the ROK public of the U.S. ironclad commitment to their defense.

*Question 7.* An opinion editorial in the Wall Street Journal recently compared current U.S. policy failures with North Korea to U.S.-Soviet Union tensions in the 1980's when the U.S. moved Pershing II medium-range ballistic missiles to bases in West Germany in response to the Soviets' growing nuclear capability. Has the administration considered other shows of force that might incentivize and stimulate China to be more active in trying to remove the Kim regime? For example, has the administration considered placing mid-range nuclear cruise missiles in Japan or South Korea to offset North Korea's possible future mid-range missile capability?

Answer. The United States has executed numerous flexible deterrence operations in 2016, both in response to the DPRK threat and in an effort to assure our South Korean allies. These operations have included, but are not limited to, B-52 and B-1 bomber flights over the Korean Peninsula, publicizing the visit of a nuclear ballistic missile submarine to Guam and inviting ROK defense officials to tour it, the agreement to deploy a THAAD battery to South Korea and the rotation of a high-end conventional capabilities like the fifth generation F-22 to Osan Air Base for joint training. Additionally, the growing threat posed by the DPRKs nuclear and ballistic capabilities has also been a central factor in fostering greater trilateral cooperation with Japan.

We believe the increased presence of U.S. strategic capabilities in Northeast Asia and the enhanced trilateral cooperation with Japan have incentivized China to work harder to constrain DPRK aggression and provocations.

*Question 8.* North Korea's nuclear cooperation with Iran is well documented. Iranian officials reportedly traveled to North Korea to witness each of its three nuclear tests—in October 2006, May 2009, and February 2013. Just before North Korea's third test, a senior American official said that "it's very possible that the North Koreans are testing for two countries." Noted North Korea expert Bruce Bechtol wrote earlier this year that "North Korea continues to supply technology, components, and even raw materials for Iran's HEU [highly-enriched uranium] weaponization program." And, Director of National Intelligence Clapper's 2015 Worldwide Threat Assessment stated that Pyongyang's "export of ballistic missiles and associated materials to several countries, including Iran and Syria, and its assistance to Syria's construction of a nuclear reactor illustrate its willingness to proliferate dangerous technologies."

- Can you inform me of the State Department's current efforts to halt this sharing of nuclear technology between North Korea and Iran? What more can be done?

- As North Korea remains strapped for cash due to sanctions, do you expect to see more efforts to sell nuclear technology and material?

Answer. The United States continues to work closely with our partners and the international community to address the threats posed by North Korea's nuclear and ballistic missile programs. The United States closely monitors and reviews all available information on North Korea's WMD programs and its proliferation activities worldwide, including any efforts to provide Iran with proliferation-sensitive materials or technologies.

We continue to take concerted steps, both unilateral and multilateral, to impede North Korea's proliferation activities, including through the imposition and enforcement of sanctions under relevant U.S. authorities, and United Nations Security Council resolutions concerning North Korea.

We also continue to closely monitor Iran's activities to ensure they are consistent with Iran's nuclear commitments under the Joint Comprehensive Plans of Action (JCPOA) and with the requirements of U.N. Security Council resolution 2231 (2015). We have been clear with Iran that the sanctions relief provided under the JCPOA is contingent on Iran's continued fulfillment of its nuclear-related commitments for their full duration.

While we cannot predict whether North Korea will increase its efforts to sell nuclear technology and material, we do know that sanctions have been effective in both limiting North Korea's access to cash and thwarting its efforts to export technology and material.

*Question 9.* Reports also suggest that North Korea has received cooperation from and has cooperated with both Russia and Syria on ballistic missile and nuclear development.

- Is the State Department aware of the transfer of any materials to or from Russia or Syria that violate U.N. sanctions and resolutions?
- Is the State Department looking into tracking this cooperation and reporting to Congress on these fronts?
- If not, what resources might State need to track this data?
- If this is classified information, would you provide me and my staff with a briefing on this topic in a classified setting?

Answer. The United States rigorously and continuously monitors North Korea's efforts to cooperate with other nations in violation of the DPRK's commitments and its obligations under U.N. Security Council Resolutions. We would be happy to provide you and your staff with a briefing on these efforts in a classified setting.

---

RESPONSES TO QUESTIONS FOR THE RECORD SUBMITTED
TO ASSISTANT SECRETARY RUSSEL BY SENATOR RUBIO

*Question 1.* It has been over two weeks since North Korea's fifth nuclear test and the best that we were able to get from the United Nations was a press statement condemning the test and pledging to work on appropriate measures. I understand that a press statement is probably the lowest level of Security Council reaction available.

- Why has the Security Council not acted to address this situation?
- Will we accept a resolution that does not eliminate the loopholes in the previous resolution?

Answer. The United States Mission to the United Nations is working with partners to achieve consensus on how to best limit importation of those North Korean exports that benefit the regime, vice those which benefits the livelihoods of everyday North Koreans. If those efforts fail to produce the desired narrowing of the UNSCR 2270 so-called "livelihood" exemption, the administration stands ready to continue high-level diplomatic engagement with all importers of North Korean coal, iron and iron ore, and consider the best way to promote global implementation of UNSCR 2270 using domestic sanctions authorities.

*Question 2.* Will we accept a resolution that does not sanction the Chinese entity and individuals we designated this week?

Answer. The United States Mission to the United Nations is working diligently to negotiate new sanctions against North Korea in response to its latest nuclear test. We are well aware that North Korea's economy is heavily dependent on China. The administration has engaged Beijing at the highest levels to seek greater Chinese cooperation on imposing costs on North Korea for its threatening behavior. We regularly urge China to do more to prevent North Korea from using Chinese companies or infrastructure in ways that can benefit the DPRK's illicit activities. At times, the administration turns to tools beyond UN sanctions, including restrictive measures like U.S. domestic sanctions, export controls, and criminal proceedings.

*Question 3.* The Center for Strategic and International Studies Beyond Parallel program reported last week that from 1994-2008 North Korea conducted 17 missile events and one nuclear test and during the Obama administration those numbers increased dramatically to 58 missile events and four nuclear tests. Now that we know China is not an honest partner in countering North Korea, what are our plans for protecting the United States and our Allies in the region against this growing threat?

Answer. Our policy is grounded in three tracks: deterrence, pressure, and diplomacy. It seeks to convince Pyongyang to return to the negotiating table and agree to complete, verifiable, and irreversible denuclearization.

To deter a North Korean attack, we maintain a strong defensive military posture, rooted in our ironclad alliances with the ROK and Japan. We consistently and publicly reaffirm our commitment to our Allies and continue to work with the ROK and Japan to develop a comprehensive set of Alliance capabilities to counter the multiple threats, including in particular the North Korean ballistic missile threat.

We have pursued a comprehensive, sustained pressure campaign—of which sanctions are a key part. The goal of this pressure is to raise the cost to North Korea for violating international law and to impede the North's ability to participate in or to fund its unlawful activities.

We are aware that North Korea's economy is heavily dependent on China. The administration has engaged Beijing at the highest levels to seek greater Chinese cooperation to impose costs on North Korea for its threatening behavior. We regularly urge China to do more to prevent North Korea from using Chinese companies or infrastructure in ways that can benefit the DPRK's illicit activities.

*Question 4.* During the September 28 SFRC Hearing you stated: "I myself am not aware of any evidence of [Iran and North Korea] cooperation currently on nuclear or missile programs." A Treasury Department press release in January 2016 stated that: Sayyed Javad Musavi, a Shahid Hemmat Industrial Group (SHIG) "commercial director ... has worked directly with North Korean officials in Iran from U.N.- and U.S.-designated Korea Mining Development Trading Corporation (KOMID). SHIG also coordinates KOMID shipments to Iran. The shipments have included valves, electronics, and measuring equipment suitable for use in ground testing of liquid propellant ballistic missiles and space launch vehicles. Within the past several years, Iranian missile technicians from SHIG traveled to North Korea to work on an 80-ton rocket booster being developed by the North Korean government." The Treasury press release also stated that Seyed Mirahmad Nooshin, the director of SHIG, and Sayyed Medhi Farahi, deputy of Iran's Ministry of Defense for Armed Forces Logistics (MODAFL), "have been critical to the development of the 80-ton rocket booster, and both traveled to Pyongyang during contract negotiations." SHIG and MODAFL are both designated by the United States.

♦ Are Iran and North Korea working together on an 80-ton ballistic missile as described in the January 2016 press release?

Answer. Our understanding of this activity is consistent with the information contained in the Treasury Department's press release issued in January 2016. For more details on any ballistic missile related cooperation between North Korea and Iran, we would recommend that you obtain a briefing from the Intelligence Community (IC).

*Question 5.* If so, have you reported this to the United Nations Security Council as a violation of Iran-related and North Korea-related resolutions?

Answer. We do not have sufficiently detailed information on this activity to provide to the UN Security Council at the required classification level. However, we continue to call attention to North Korea and Iran's ballistic missile related activities at the United Nations. For example, we reported Iran's March 2016 missile launches to the Security Council and requested the Council review this matter to determine an appropriate response. With regard to North Korea, we are currently working to reach agreement on another UNSCR targeting its weapons of mass destruction (WMD) and ballistic missile-related proliferation programs. Such efforts help raise awareness among other governments of Iran and North Korea's missile development efforts and raise the political costs to these countries for provocative missile-related activities.

*Question 6.* Have you or do you intend to submit Sayyed Javad Musavi, Seyed Mirahmad Nooshin, and Sayyed Medhi Farahi for designation under UN Security Council Resolution 1718?

Answer. We have an ongoing process in place to identify proliferation-related entities and individuals and to recommend them to the UN Security Council 1718 Committee for designation. These individuals will be evaluated as part of that process.

*Question 7.* If not, why did the Obama administration designate these individuals?

Answer. Sayyed Javad Musavi was designated pursuant to E.O. 13382 because he provided or attempted to provide financial, material, technological, or other support for, or goods or services in support of, Iran's Shahid Hemmat Industrial Group (SHIG).

Seyed Mirahmad Nooshin was designated pursuant to E.O. 13382 for acting or purporting to act for or on behalf of SHIG, and because he provided, or attempted to provide, financial, material, technological, or other support for, or goods or services in support of, SHIG.

Farahi was designated pursuant to E.O. 13382 for acting or purporting to act for or on behalf of Iran's Ministry of Defense Armed Forces Logistics (MODAFL), and because he provided, or attempted to provide, financial, material, technological, or other support for, or goods or services in support of, MODAFL.

*Question 8.* Was this an effort to answer critics of the Joint Comprehensive Plan of Action that the United States has not acted against Iran's ballistic missile activities?

Answer. Our resolve to counter Iran's ballistic missile program and other destabilizing regional activities has not changed since the JCPOA entered into effect. We continue to use a wide range of multilateral and unilateral tools to counter Iran's ballistic missile development efforts, including disrupting and interdicting missile technology going to or from Iran.

*Question 9.* Have you initiated an investigation of Sayyed Javad Musavi, Seyed Mirahmad Nooshin, and Sayyed Medhi Farahi as required by Section 102 of the North Korea Sanctions and Policy Enhancement Act of 2016 (P.L. 114–122)?

Answer. The functions and authorities under section 102(a) regarding initiation of investigations pursuant to the North Korea Sanctions and Policy Enhancement Act of 2016 (the Act) were delegated to the Secretary of the Treasury. For questions regarding current investigations under this section, we refer you to the Department of the Treasury.

*Question 10.* If so, why have these individuals not been designated as required by the mandatory sanctions in P.L. 114–122? If not, why?

Please provide a reason why the Obama administration has not provided a waiver of the requirement to impose sanctions under the North Korea Sanctions and Policy Enhancement Act of 2016 (PL 114-122) for the following individuals:

Sayyed Javad Musavi

Seyed Mirahmad Nooshin

Sayyed Medhi Farahi

Answer. We cannot comment on future potential designations. However, please note that these individuals have already been designated under E.O. 13382, resulting in the blocking of their property and interests in the United States.

*Question 11.* Given that the IAEA has no visibility into the North Korean nuclear program and our own poor track record in catching North Korean nuclear cooperation with other rogue actors early, what tools do we have in place to ensure that Iran is not continuing its prohibited nuclear activities inside North Korea?

Answer. Despite the DPRK's expulsion of IAEA inspectors from North Korea in 2009, the IAEA has continued to monitor the DPRK's nuclear activities and keep Member States informed of developments in the DPRK's nuclear program through the Director General's annual reports.

The IAEA also remains dedicated to maintaining its readiness to resume its monitoring and verification presence in the DPRK, efforts on which the IAEA has the United States' full and steadfast support.

The United States continues to work closely with our partners and the international community to address the threats posed by North Korea's nuclear and ballistic missile programs. We continue to take concerted steps, both unilaterally and multilaterally, to impede North Korea's proliferation activities, including through the imposition and enforcement of sanctions under relevant U.S. authorities and UN Security Council resolutions and by urging all countries to implement UN Security Council resolutions concerning the DPRK.

We also continue to do the same with respect to Iran, both unilaterally and multilaterally, in accordance with UNSCR 2231 (2015) and the provisions of the Joint Comprehensive Plans of Action (JCPOA).

We are committed to ensuring that Iran fulfills all of its nuclear-related commitments in a verifiable and complete manner. Because there is comprehensive IAEA monitoring of the entire fuel cycle within Iran, we are confident we will know if Iran attempts to cheat, including through the introduction of foreign technology or material into Iran's nuclear fuel cycle that is contrary to the JCPOA.

*Question 12.* Are you working to coordinate investigations with China, Japan, and South Korea? If not, do you commit to do so?

Answer. We reviewed media articles released in August 2016 claiming David Sneddon, a U.S. citizen who went missing from the Tiger Leaping Gorge area of China's Yunnan province since some time after August 10, 2004, had been kidnapped by the DPRK regime and was alive in Pyongyang. The U.S. Consulate in Chengdu has been in regular contact with regional Chinese officials since David Sneddon was reported missing in August 2004. We have spoken with officials from the South Korean and Japanese governments. We have also contacted the DPRK government regarding the media reports, but received no official response. Thus far, we have not been able to verify any of the information suggesting that Sneddon was abducted by North Korean officials or is alive in North Korea, but we will continue our efforts to search for any verifiable information.

*Question 13.* When is the last time you raised this case with China? What was the reaction?

Answer. Senior officials at our Embassy in Beijing and at the U.S. Consulate in Chengdu have consistently discussed the disappearance of David Sneddon with Chinese officials. Most recently, in September 2016, Consulate Chengdu sent a diplomatic note to Chinese officials seeking any additional information about his case. In response, Chinese officials reported that China continues to devote resources to the search for Mr. Sneddon, but no progress has been made. This remains an open missing person case in China, thus a death certificate has not been issued. The Department of State has not been able to verify any of the information suggesting that Sneddon is alive in North Korea, but continue our efforts to search for any verifiable information.

*Question 14.* In June a North Korean agent was captured by Chinese officials in Dandong with $5 million in counterfeit $100 bills. Are we seeing an increase in North Korea's efforts to counterfeit currency?

Answer. We take all efforts by North Korea to evade U.S. and international sanctions seriously. In order to check these attempts, the U.S. has used domestic sanctions to highlight these activities, consistent with the North Korea Sanctions Policy and Enhancement Act. For more information about activities specific to countering the threat of counterfeit currency, we refer you to the U.S. Secret Service.

*Question 15.* What are we doing to stop this and other DPRK illicit activities?

Answer. We are well aware that DPRK officials and other nationals are engaged in many illicit activities around the globe. Whenever we become aware of such activities, we work with like-minded partners including the ROK and Japan to alert the host country. We then press the host country to take appropriate action, including law enforcement measures or, in the case of individuals with diplomatic immunity, removing them from the country.

*Question 16.* Are we working with China to understand whether North Korea has used other counterfeit U.S. currency inside China?

Answer. Our cooperation and dialogue with China in reference to North Korea's unacceptable and destabilizing activity is wide ranging. For questions regarding North Korea's use of counterfeit currency, we refer you to the U.S. Secret Service.

*Question 17.* Executive Order 13551 provides a mechanism for designation of those who counterfeit U.S. currency, are we preparing to designate the North Korean agent arrested in China?

Answer. We take all efforts by North Korea to evade U.S. and international sanctions seriously. Any ongoing investigations in connection with this activity would be undertaken by the Department of Treasury.

*Question 18.* A recent press article described brokers who lure or abduct North Korean women and bring them to China where they are then sold into marriages in China. These women fear both the North Korean regime for its brutality and that China or North Korean agents will return them back to North Korea. Have we raised this issue with China? Are we pressing Beijing to stop sending North Korean refugees back to the brutal Kim regime?

The Report of the Commission of Inquiry on Human Rights in the DPRK in February 2014 recommended: "The Security Council should refer the situation in the Democratic People's Republic of Korea to the International Criminal Court for action in accordance with that court's jurisdiction. The Security Council should also adopt targeted sanctions against those who appear to be most responsible for crimes against humanity."

Answer. The State Department continues to encourage the Government of China at the highest levels to provide appropriate protections for victims of human trafficking, including those arriving from the DPRK. Secretary Kerry has raised our concerns with Chinese officials on multiple occasions, including at the annual Strategic and Economic Dialogue, and Ambassador Coppedge will travel to China later this year to continue our efforts to improve China's anti-trafficking practices and facilities.

*Question 19.* Has China blocked the Security Council's referral of the DPRK to the International Criminal Court?

Answer. No, China has not blocked the Security Council's referral of the DPRK to the International Criminal Court.

*Question 20.* If so, when will the United States publicly force China to veto the referral and once and for all reveal that it is covering for this brutal regime?

Answer. The State Department regularly evaluates the human rights abuses committed by the DPRK and continuously reviews appropriate measures to address them via the United Nations.

*Question 21.* Also related to North Korean refugees, we're hearing from sources on the ground in China that the Chinese are repatriating North Koreans and raising bounties for turning in North Koreans. We've even heard reports that Chinese officials are processing asylum seekers for the North Korean government who then immediately sends them to labor camps or worse. Can you confirm this? What are we doing to press China on this issue?

Answer. We are aware of reports prior to April 2015 stating that Chinese authorities were forcibly repatriating North Korean refugees by treating them as illegal economic migrants. There were no reports of the forced repatriation of North Koreans between April 2015 and March 2016—the latest time period for which confirmed data is available—but media outlets have reported a resurgence of repatriations in recent months, which we have not yet verified.

We will continue to urge China to uphold its commitments with regard to North Korean refugees as a state party to the 1951 Convention on the Status of Refugees and its 1967 Protocol.

We are in regular touch with the ROK government on this issue. The ROK routinely asks us to avoid publicizing defector cases, as it makes it more difficult to get them safely to the ROK. ROK officials have said they are satisfied with Chinese cooperation on defectors and are not aware of any new cases of forced repatriation. We continue to encourage the Government of China to provide protections for victims of human trafficking and refugees, including those arriving from the DPRK.

*Question 22.* A growing problem is North Korea's export of slave labor which constitutes a grave human rights abuse and also serves as a source of cash flow to the regime. What is the Department doing to stop the trafficking of North Korean laborers for hard currency?

Answer. North Korea's export of labor generates significant revenue for the DPRK government and enables the development of its illicit nuclear and missile programs. Under Executive Order 13722, the Department of Treasury, in consultation with the Department of State, has authority to designate individuals and entities determined to be responsible for the exportation of workers from North Korea. We work closely with other governments to document and disseminate information about the living and working conditions of North Korean workers in the DPRK and overseas. We have also raised our concerns with governments around the world about the use of DPRK workers in their countries, and some governments have modified their policies. As our efforts in these countries demonstrate, our embassies around the world are deeply engaged with host governments on the issue of DPRK laborers and the revenue they generate for the regime.

--------

RESPONSES TO QUESTIONS FOR THE RECORD SUBMITTED
TO ASSISTANT SECRETARY RUSSEL BY SENATOR GARDNER

*Question 1.* On March 18, 2016, New York Times reported they uncovered documents, which showed how a ZTE, a Chinese firm, "would set up seemingly independent companies—called 'cut-off companies'—that would sign the deals in other countries. That could enable it to continue to do business in Iran, North Korea and other countries placed under American restrictions."

On June 2, 2016, New York Times reported that the U.S. Commerce Department is also investigating the Chinese company Huawei, including demanding that the company "turn over all information regarding the export or re-export of American technology to Cuba, Iran, North Korea, Sudan and Syria, according to a subpoena sent to Huawei and viewed by The New York Times. The subpoena is part of an investigation into whether Huawei broke United States export controls."

♦ What are ZTE and Huawei's dealings with North Korea?

♦ Are North Korean nationals, or individuals working at the behest of the North Korean regime, utilizing any Huawei or ZTE equipment to conduct cyberattacks?

Answer. We do not comment on ongoing investigations. Generally speaking, the recent Executive Order signed by President Obama (EO 13722) imposed prohibitions on the exportation from the U.S. or the re-exportation from abroad of goods, services, and technology to North Korean entities, except where licensed by the Commerce or Treasury Department, as appropriate. In addition, Commerce has long required licenses for all exports and reexports, except for food and medicine, to North Korea. We refer you to the Treasury and Commerce Departments for more information about their efforts.

EO 13722 also authorizes new sanctions designations for those engaging in significant activities undermining cybersecurity against targets outside of North Korea on behalf of the Government North Korea or the Workers' Party of Korea. This includes the ability to impose sanctions on persons providing material assistance, sponsorship, or financial, material, or technological support for, or goods and services to or in support of any person undermining or attempting to undermine cybersecurity on behalf of the Government of North Korea or the Korean Workers Party. This authority is consistent with those outlined in the North Korea Sanctions Policy Enhancement Act.

Dealings with North Korea by ZTE and Huawei is a topic that would be best addressed via an interagency briefing in a classified setting after the investigation has concluded.

*Question 2.* If there is evidence that ZTE or Huawei have collaborated with the North Korean regime to conduct illicit activities, would you support their designation under the North Korea Sanctions and Policy Enhancement Act or any other legal authorities?

Answer. We do not comment on ongoing investigations. We have used our sanctions authorities and other restrictive measures against third-country nationals and entities, including Chinese. For example, on September 26, 2016, the Treasury Department imposed sanctions on four Chinese nationals and one Chinese entity that were found to be supporting North Korea's WMD proliferation activities.

We will continue to use all tools at our disposal in order to halt North Korea's nuclear proliferation activities, deprive the Kim regime of hard currency, and protect the United States from threats to our national security.

---

RESPONSES TO QUESTIONS FOR THE RECORD SUBMITTED
TO ASSISTANT SECRETARY RUSSEL BY SENATOR PERDUE

*Question 1.* The importance of China's role in enforcement of these sanctions cannot be overstated. Between 2011 and 2015, more than 90% of North Korea's trade with the outside world is believed to have been with China and South Korea. Can you describe the administration's current efforts to influence China to leverage its relationship with North Korea (DPRK) to fully implement sanctions?

Answer. The administration has engaged Beijing at the highest levels to seek greater Chinese cooperation in imposing costs on North Korea for its threatening behavior. We regularly urge China to do more to prevent North Korea from using Chinese companies or infrastructure in ways that can benefit the DPRK's illicit activities. All options, including sanctions, remain on the table. We are not shying away from their use.

On September 26, the Treasury Department and the Justice Department moved in concert to check the sanctions evasion activities undertaken by a Chinese entity and four Chinese nationals: Dandong Hongxiang Industrial Development Company Ltd (DHID), Ma Xiaohong, Zhou Jianshu, Hong Jinhua, and Luo Chuanxu. The Treasury Department added these persons to the Specially Designated Nationals List, while the Justice Department unsealed criminal charges against the same for conspiring to evade U.S. economic sanctions and violating OFAC's Weapons of Mass Destruction Proliferators Sanctions Regulations as well as conspiracy to launder money.

We will continue to urge China to exert its leverage as North Korea's largest trading partner. We seek to force Kim Jong Un come to the realization that the only viable path forward for his country is denuclearization.

*Question 2.* The UN Sanctions Committee has difficulty with collecting the data necessary to properly enforce sanctions against North Korea. A major reason analysts give for this is that it is broadly suspected that China's border with North Korea is significantly porous, allowing any flow of goods between the two countries to go undocumented. Is the administration looking into ways to influence China to a) fully comply with reporting requirements under DPRK sanctions, and b) to begin to enforce their border with North Korea more stringently?

Answer. We agree that more work is needed to limit the flow of illicit goods over the China-North Korea border and we continue to work closely with the Chinese to achieve greater cooperation and application of pressure on North Korea. While we are aware of China's concerns that pressure on North Korea could precipitate a destabilizing crisis, we consider North Korea's nuclear and missile programs as posing a far greater threat to regional security. We acknowledge steps China has taken to implement UN sanctions but have repeatedly urged China to improve its implementation and apply pressure needed to effect a change in North Korea's behavior.

China has objected to U.S. actions intended to strengthen our defenses against North Korean military threats to ourselves and our allies, but we have made clear that we will take all necessary steps to deter and defend against those threats. We closely coordinate with China on sanctions and other measures to counter North Korea's problematic behavior.

*Question 3.* We also know that UN sanctions have, in some ways, had the perverse effect of actually boosting revenue flows to North Korea. Due to certain sanctions exemptions, such as those allowing the importation of goods from North Korea when the profits from such imports are generated "for the people's livelihood," trade with China and South Korea has increased by 90% in 2011. Further, China has exploited these exemptions to increase their North Korean imports of irons and iron ore by 64 percent. However, certification that these imports comply with sanctions exemptions are enforced by China's own custom's authorities, creating a significant conflict of interest.

♦ How has the administration gone about addressing the issue of exemptions with China?

♦ Has the administration discussed the possibility of defining "for the people's livelihood" exemption with the Sanctions Committee or with China? If so, how?

♦ Alternatively, has the administration sought to persuade China to raise the bar for businesses seeking to take advantage of the "livelihoods" exception by requiring some type of documentation? If so, what kind? Would there be any possibility of an oversight mechanism outside of Chinese customs authorities?

Answer. The administration is deeply troubled by the increase in the exports of North Korean coal to China, including under the "livelihood" exception. Not only is North Korean coal in many cases mined by essentially enslaved workers—including children—it helps to prop up the Kim regime at the expense of everyday North Koreans, making coal harder to obtain for those seeking to heat their homes and cook their food.

We are taking immediate steps to address this problem. Specifically, the U.S. Mission to the United Nations in New York is seeking ways to limit DPRK exports of coal that benefit the regime. If those efforts fail to produce the desired narrowing of the UNSCR 2270 livelihoods exception, the administration stands ready to continue high-level diplomatic engagement with all importers of North Korean coal, iron and iron ore, and consider the best way to promote stronger and global implementation of UNSCR 2270, potentially including by using domestic sanctions authorities.

*Question 4.* A key question for implementation of sanctions continues to be whether China will inspect shipments on its border, through its ports, and in its air space, for shipments of illicit goods and materials to and from North Korea. China is not a participant in the Proliferation Security Initiative (PSI), which holds regular information-sharing and ship-boarding exercises to improve international coordination and facilitate timely interdictions. Has the administration explored increasing cooperation with other PSI countries, namely at key transshipment points, to improve intelligence collection and information sharing on illicit shipments to and from North Korea?

Answer. North Korea's economy is indeed heavily dependent on China. The administration has engaged Beijing at the highest levels to seek greater Chinese cooperation on imposing costs on North Korea for its threatening behavior. We regularly urge China to do more to prevent North Korea from using Chinese companies or infrastructure in ways that can benefit the DPRK's illicit activities. At times, the administration turns to other tools, including restrictive measures like sanctions, export controls, and criminal proceedings.

We have seen the report by Asan Institute and C4ADS, which shines light on North Korea's overseas networks. In addition to the recent DHID-related designations, State and Treasury have also taken steps to curb North Korea's shipping operations. Specifically, Treasury designated Ocean Maritime Management (OMM) and several of its front companies; OMM is highlighted in a recent report by the

Asan Institute and C4ADS as being a key conduit of North Korean overseas activity. The administration has also identified as blocked 18 vessels connected to OMM.

Furthermore, the administration secured the listing of 31 vessels controlled or operated by OMM in UNSCR 2270, along with many new maritime sanctions authorities that better enable a global campaign to shut down North Korea's maritime activities. The administration is also seeking to further strengthen U.N. sanctions in this realm. The Department of State has led diplomatic efforts to ensure the implementation of U.N. obligations on Member States related to prohibitions on flagging, owning, and operating DPRK-affiliated vessels.

PSI partners in the region have hosted several bilateral and multilateral events, workshops, and exercises. In September 2016, the third annual PSI Asia-Pacific Exercise Rotation (PSI-APER) event was held in Singapore, which included an at-sea live boarding exercise, an in-port interdiction demonstration, and a tabletop exercise and policy discussion. A key focus of the tabletop exercise was on the importance of timely and accurate intelligence and information to fulfill commitments that countries make when they endorse the PSI Statement of Interdiction Principles. These commitments include undertaking "effective measures, either alone or in concert with other states, for interdicting the transfer or transport of WMD, their delivery systems, and related materials to and from states and non-state actors of proliferation concern." Australia will host the next PSI APER event in 2017.

*Question 5.* Why has Treasury not yet cut off North Korea, financial institutions that facilitate transactions for the government, as well as third parties that use those institutions, from any access to the U.S. financial system? In June of this year, the Treasury Department announced its finding that DPRK is a jurisdiction of primary money laundering concern. At the same time, Treasury also released a notice of proposed rulemaking recommending a special measure to prohibit covered U.S. financial institutions from opening or maintaining correspondent accounts with North Korea financial institutions, and prohibiting the use of U.S. correspondent accounts to process transactions for North Korean institutions.

♦ What is keeping Treasury from implementing this rule?

♦ What steps is the administration taking to educate U.S. financial institutions about this new policy?

♦ Has Treasury considered also targeting third-party banks that use those financial messaging services?

Answer. We believe that the Section 311 final rule regarding North Korea will be an important step in further isolating North Korea from the international financial system, despite the fact that it was already one of the most heavily sanctioned countries. In addition to being consistent with the North Korea Sanctions and Policy Enhancement Act, it would also amplify the sanctions imposed by United Nations Security Council Resolution (UNSCR) 2270, which was passed on March 2, 2016. Among other significant restrictions, UNSCR 2270 requires Member States to sever correspondent banking relationships with North Korean financial institutions by May 31, 2016.

While North Korea's financial institutions do not maintain correspondent accounts with U.S. financial institutions, the North Korean government continues to use state-controlled financial institutions and front companies to surreptitiously conduct illicit international financial transactions, some of which support the proliferation of weapons of mass destruction and the development of ballistic missiles. While current U.S. law already generally prohibits U.S. financial institutions from engaging in both direct and indirect transactions with North Korean financial institutions, we anticipate that the final rule under Section 311 will support international sanctions already in place against North Korea and provide greater protection for the U.S. financial system from North Korean illicit activity.

While we cannot comment publicly on future sanctions actions, we can assure you that we will continue working with our international partners to cut off services to North Korea's banking sector.

*Question 6* After DPRK conducted its 5th nuclear test, the U.S. flew several B1 stealth bombers over South Korea as a showcase of our military force. In your opinion, have these flights had an effect in North Korea's decision-making?

Answer. Yes. The B1 bomber flights had two purposes. First, to deter DPRK aggression and second, to assure the ROK public. The two separate B1 flights in September demonstrated both the regular availability and rapid responsiveness of U.S. strategic capabilities and was intended to deter DPRK aggression against the ROK and Japan. The U.S. ability to project power onto the Korean Peninsula was a signal that was heavily publicized and successfully communicated to the DPRK through USG press releases. These flights were also designed to assure the ROK public of the U.S. ironclad commitment to their defense.

*Question 7.* An opinion editorial in the Wall Street Journal recently compared current U.S. policy failures with North Korea to U.S.-Soviet Union tensions in the 1980's when the U.S. moved Pershing II medium-range ballistic missiles to bases in West Germany in response to the Soviets' growing nuclear capability. Has the administration considered other shows of force that might incentivize and stimulate China to be more active in trying to remove the Kim regime? For example, has the administration considered placing mid-range nuclear cruise missiles in Japan or South Korea to offset North Korea's possible future mid-range missile capability?

Answer. The United States has executed numerous flexible deterrence operations in 2016, both in response to the DPRK threat and in an effort to assure our South Korean allies. These operations have included, but are not limited to, B-52 and B-1 bomber flights over the Korean Peninsula, publicizing the visit of a nuclear ballistic missile submarine to Guam and inviting ROK defense officials to tour it, the agreement to deploy a THAAD battery to South Korea and the rotation of a high-end conventional capabilities like the fifth generation F-22 to Osan Air Base for joint training. Additionally, the growing threat posed by the DPRKs nuclear and ballistic capabilities has also been a central factor in fostering greater trilateral cooperation with Japan.

We believe the increased presence of U.S. strategic capabilities in Northeast Asia and the enhanced trilateral cooperation with Japan have incentivized China to work harder to constrain DPRK aggression and provocations.

*Question 8.* North Korea's nuclear cooperation with Iran is well documented. Iranian officials reportedly traveled to North Korea to witness each of its three nuclear tests—in October 2006, May 2009, and February 2013. Just before North Korea's third test, a senior American official said that "it's very possible that the North Koreans are testing for two countries." Noted North Korea expert Bruce Bechtol wrote earlier this year that "North Korea continues to supply technology, components, and even raw materials for Iran's HEU [highly-enriched uranium] weaponization program." And, Director of National Intelligence Clapper's 2015 Worldwide Threat Assessment stated that Pyongyang's "export of ballistic missiles and associated materials to several countries, including Iran and Syria, and its assistance to Syria's construction of a nuclear reactor ...illustrate its willingness to proliferate dangerous technologies."

♦ Can you inform me of the State Department's current efforts to halt this sharing of nuclear technology between North Korea and Iran? What more can be done?

♦ As North Korea remains strapped for cash due to sanctions, do you expect to see more efforts to sell nuclear technology and material?

Answer. The United States continues to work closely with our partners and the international community to address the threats posed by North Korea's nuclear and ballistic missile programs. The United States closely monitors and reviews all available information on North Korea's WMD programs and its proliferation activities worldwide, including any efforts to provide Iran with proliferation-sensitive materials or technologies.

We continue to take concerted steps, both unilateral and multilateral, to impede North Korea's proliferation activities, including through the imposition and enforcement of sanctions under relevant U.S. authorities, and United Nations Security Council resolutions concerning North Korea.

We also continue to closely monitor Iran's activities to ensure they are consistent with Iran's nuclear commitments under the Joint Comprehensive Plans of Action (JCPOA) and with the requirements of U.N. Security Council resolution 2231 (2015). We have been clear with Iran that the sanctions relief provided under the JCPOA is contingent on Iran's continued fulfillment of its nuclear-related commitments for their full duration.

While we cannot predict whether North Korea will increase its efforts to sell nuclear technology and material, we do know that sanctions have been effective in both limiting North Korea's access to cash and thwarting its efforts to export technology and material.

*Question 9.* Reports also suggest that North Korea has received cooperation from and has cooperated with both Russia and Syria on ballistic missile and nuclear development.

♦ Is the State Department aware of the transfer of any materials to or from Russia or Syria that violate U.N. sanctions and resolutions?

♦ Is the State Department looking into tracking this cooperation and reporting to Congress on these fronts?

♦ If not, what resources might State need to track this data?

♦ If this is classified information, would you be provide me and my staff with a briefing on this topic in a classified setting?

Answer. The United States rigorously and continuously monitors North Korea's efforts to cooperate with other nations in violation of the DPRK's commitments and its obligations under U.N. Security Council Resolutions. We would be happy to provide you and your staff with a briefing on these efforts in a classified setting.

○